Antipasti

APPETIZERS

$\mathbb{A}$*ntipasto* (to use the singular form) is merely the Italian equivalent of the French *hors d'oeuvre,* or appetizer, in English. These may be as simple as you wish, or as elaborate and extensive as the particular occasion dictates.

The traditional selection of *antipasto* includes some of the following: a few slices of salami and *mortadella* (that delicious type of bologna), several shrimp, slices of cheese, olives, stuffed eggplant or peppers, prosciutto, *bresaola,* baked clams, radishes, sardines, but of course, these are only suggestions. The various *antipasti* which appear in this section of the book may be served as separate first courses, if you wish. Some of them are ideal for serving to guests with a pre-dinner drink, should you desire.

It is of particular interest to mention the origin of the word *antipasto. Pasta* is the Italian word which covers all of the various dough preparations (like spaghetti, macaroni, ravioli, and so forth) that form an integral part of so many Italian meals. *Antipasto,* thus, literally means "before the pasta," the appetizer served before the *pasta* course.

1

Vongole Reganate

BAKED CLAMS

36 hard shell clams
¼ cup finely chopped parsley
2 cloves garlic, minced
¼ cup grated Parmesan cheese
¼ teaspoon freshly ground black pepper
½ teaspoon oregano
¼ cup olive oil
¼ cup dry bread crumbs

Scrub the clams under cold running water until shells are shiny. Dry, then place in a skillet. Cover and place over low heat until shells open. Discard the top shells. Arrange the clams on the half shell in a baking dish. Sprinkle with a mixture of the parsley, garlic, cheese, pepper and oregano, then sprinkle with the oil and finally the bread crumbs. Bake in a 425° oven 5 minutes. Serve immediately.

SERVES : 4–6

Note: Mussels (*cozze*) may be prepared in the same manner.

Legumi in Aceto

PICKLED VEGETABLES

12 small white onions
1 small cauliflower, in flowerets
½ pound small mushroom caps
2 green peppers, cut in ½-inch strips
18 black olives
1 cup olive oil
1½ cups wine vinegar
2 teaspoons salt
¾ teaspoon freshly ground black pepper
4 tablespoons sugar
1 clove garlic, minced

Toss together the onions, cauliflower, mushrooms, green peppers and olives. Bring to a boil the oil, vinegar, salt, pepper, sugar and garlic. Cool 5 minutes and pour over the vegetables. Cover and marinate for at least 24 hours in the refrigerator. Drain and serve with antipasto or pierce with cocktail picks.

SERVES : 6–8

Insalata di Scampi e Funghi

SHRIMP AND MUSHROOM APPETIZER

1 pound firm white mushrooms
½ cup olive oil
4 tablespoons lemon juice
½ teaspoon freshly ground black pepper
⅛ teaspoon minced garlic
1 pound cooked cleaned shrimp
1¼ teaspoons salt
2 tablespoons minced parsley

Wash and dry the mushrooms. Remove the stems and use for another purpose. Slice the caps paper thin; add the oil, lemon juice, pepper and garlic. Marinate in the refrigerator 2 hours, mixing frequently.

Thirty minutes before serving, mix in the shrimp and salt. Taste for seasoning. Sprinkle with the parsley.

SERVES : 4–6

Carciofi alla Certosina

STUFFED ARTICHOKES WITH TUNA

8 artichokes
1 7¾-ounce can tuna fish, drained and flaked
1 can anchovy fillets, minced
2 tablespoons chopped capers
¼ cup chopped parsley
¼ teaspoon black pepper
1 clove garlic, minced
¼ cup coarse bread crumbs
½ cup olive oil

Buy young, tender artichokes.

Remove the stems of the artichokes and with a scissor, trim the pointed ends of the leaves. Wash carefully. Cook in boiling salted water 10 minutes; drain and press the leaves open downward on a solid surface. Remove the chokes (fuzzy centers) with a sharp knife or spoon.

Mix together the tuna fish, anchovies, capers, parsley, pepper and garlic. Put some of the mixture in the centers and between the leaves of the artichokes. Arrange in an upright position in a heavy saucepan. Sprinkle with the bread crumbs. Pour 1 tablespoon oil over each, then add water to the saucepan to a depth of ¼-inch. Cover the pot and cook over low heat 40 minutes. Add a little boiling water if necessary. Serve hot or cold.

SERVES : 8

Funghi alla Parmigiana

CHEESE-STUFFED MUSHROOMS

2 pounds mushrooms
½ cup grated Parmesan cheese
¾ cup dry bread crumbs
½ cup grated onions
2 cloves garlic, minced
3 tablespoons minced parsley
1 teaspoon salt
½ teaspoon freshly ground black pepper
½ teaspoon oregano
¾ cup olive oil

Buy large, even-sized mushrooms. Wash but do not peel them. Remove the stems and chop; mix with the cheese, bread crumbs, onions, garlic, parsley, salt, pepper and oregano. Stuff the mushroom caps.

Pour a little oil into a baking pan. Arrange the mushrooms in it. Pour the remaining oil over them, being sure to get a little on each mushroom. Bake in a 350° oven 25 minutes. Serve as an antipasto, appetizer or vegetable.

SERVES : 6–8

Funghi Ripieni con Peperoni

PEPPER-STUFFED MUSHROOMS

24 large mushrooms
4 tablespoons olive oil
¼ cup chopped onions
1 clove garlic, minced
½ cup chopped green pepper
½ teaspoon salt
¼ teaspoon black pepper
3 tablespoons grated Parmesan cheese
3 tablespoons chopped capers
1 tablespoon bread crumbs

Wash and dry the mushrooms. Remove the stems and chop fine. Heat 2 tablespoons oil in a skillet; sauté the onions, garlic and green pepper 5 minutes. Add the chopped mushroom stems; sauté 5 minutes. Mix in the salt, pepper, cheese, capers and bread crumbs; stuff the mushrooms. Place in an oiled baking dish and sprinkle with the remaining oil. Bake in a 375° oven 15 minutes.

SERVES : 6

Cappelle di Funghi Ripiene

STUFFED MUSHROOM CAPS

2 pounds firm white mushrooms
4 tablespoons olive oil
4 tablespoons butter
1 clove garlic, minced
1 tablespoon flour
¼ cup dry white wine
1 teaspoon salt
¼ teaspoon freshly ground black pepper
1 egg yolk, beaten
½ cup dry bread crumbs

Wash and dry the mushrooms; remove the stems and chop them. Heat 1 tablespoon oil and 1 tablespoon butter in a skillet; sauté the mushrooms and garlic 2 minutes. Blend in the flour, and add the wine, salt and pepper. Cook over medium heat 5 minutes, stirring frequently. All the liquid should be evaporated; if it is not, raise heat to dry. Cool 10 minutes, then mix in the egg yolk. Stuff the mushroom caps.

Pour the remaining oil into a shallow baking dish; arrange the mushrooms in it. Sprinkle with the bread crumbs and dot with the remaining butter. Bake in a 375° oven 15 minutes. Serve hot or cold.

SERVES : 6–8

Melanzane Ripiene

STUFFED EGGPLANT

2 medium eggplants
6 tablespoons olive oil
½ cup chopped onions
½ cup peeled chopped tomatoes
1 teaspoon salt
½ teaspoon freshly ground black pepper
3 tablespoons dry bread crumbs
2 anchovy fillets, minced
2 tablespoons capers
¼ cup sliced black olives
¼ teaspoon oregano
3 tablespoons grated Parmesan cheese

Wash and dry the eggplants; remove the stems. Cut in half lengthwise; scoop out the pulp and chop. Reserve shells.

Heat 2 tablespoons oil in a skillet; sauté the onions 5 minutes. Add the eggplant, pulp; sauté 5 minutes. Add the tomatoes, salt and pepper; cook 10 minutes. Mix in the bread crumbs, anchovies, capers, olives, oregano and 2 tablespoons oil. Taste for seasoning.

Stuff the shells. Place in a baking dish or casserole. Sprinkle

with the remaining oil and the cheese. Cover, and bake in a 375°
oven 50 minutes, removing the cover for the last 15 minutes.
Serve hot or cold.

SERVES : 4

Melanzane Piccanti

SPICY EGGPLANT

2 pounds eggplant
2 teaspoons salt
4 tablespoons olive oil
1 cup thinly sliced onions
2 tablespoons chopped parsley
¼ teaspoon basil
¼ teaspoon freshly ground black pepper
1 pound tomatoes, peeled and chopped
⅛ cup wine vinegar

If possible, buy small eggplants.
Wash the eggplant (don't peel) and cut into ½-inch cubes.
Sprinkle with 1 teaspoon salt and let stand while preparing the
sauce.
Heat half the oil in a saucepan; sauté the onions 10 minutes.
Add the parsley, basil, pepper, tomatoes and remaining salt.
Bring to a boil and cook over low heat 30 minutes. Taste for
seasoning.
Drain the eggplant cubes. Heat the remaining oil in a skillet;
brown the cubes in it on all sides. Pour the vinegar over it, mix
and transfer to a serving dish. Pour the tomato sauce over it.
Serve hot or cold.

SERVES : 4–6

Peperoni Ripieni

STUFFED PEPPERS

2 slices white bread, trimmed
½ cup milk
6 green peppers
1 7¾-ounce can tuna fish
½ teaspoon salt
⅛ teaspoon freshly ground black pepper
½ cup peeled chopped tomatoes
¾ cup sliced black olives
¼ cup olive oil

Soak the bread in the milk 10 minutes. Drain and mash smooth. Cut a 1-inch piece off the stem end of the peppers; scoop out the seeds and fibres.

Drain and flake the tuna fish; mix in the bread, salt, pepper, tomatoes and olives. Taste for seasoning. Stuff the peppers and arrange in an oiled baking dish. Sprinkle peppers with oil. Cover dish; bake in a 350° oven 50 minutes or until peppers are tender. Serve hot or cold.

SERVES : 6

Peperonata con Olive e Acciughe

PEPPERS AND OLIVES

6 large red or green peppers
½ teaspoon salt
½ cup olive oil
1½ cups pitted Italian or Greek olives
2 cloves garlic, minced
6 anchovy fillets, minced

Broil the peppers as close to the heat as possible, until the skins turn black. Rub off the skins; cut the peppers into narrow strips, discarding the seeds and fibres. Sprinkle with the salt.

Heat the oil in a skillet; sauté the peppers 2 minutes. Mix in the olives, garlic and anchovies; cook 2 minutes. Serve hot.

SERVES : 6–12 as part of an *antipasto*.

Peperoni alla Piemontese

PEPPERS WITH ANCHOVY SAUCE,
PIEDMONT FASHION

6 green peppers
1 tablespoon butter
3 tablespoons olive oil
1 whole clove garlic
8 anchovy fillets, minced

Wash the peppers, cover with water and bring to a boil. Let stand 10 minutes. Drain and peel off the skin. Cut the peppers into thin slices, discarding the seeds and fibres.

Heat the butter and oil in a skillet. Add the garlic and anchovies. Cook over low heat 2 minutes, stirring constantly. Discard the garlic and pour the undrained anchovies over the peppers. Cool. Serve as an antipasto.

SERVES : 4–6

Peperoni con Acciughe

PEPPER APPETIZER

6 green and red peppers
1½ cups peeled cubed tomatoes
3 cloves garlic, sliced
½ cup minced anchovies
3 tablespoons dry bread crumbs
3 tablespoons olive oil
4 tablespoons butter

Red and green peppers may be used or all green or red. Cut the peppers in quarters lengthwise; scoop out the seeds and fibres.

Mix together the tomatoes, garlic, anchovies, bread crumbs and oil. Stuff the pepper quarters. Arrange in an oiled baking pan; dot with the butter. Bake in a 375° oven 30 minutes or until crisp but tender. Serve cold.

SERVES : 6 or 12 as part of an *antipasto*.

Funghi all'Olio

MARINATED MUSHROOMS

1 pound small button mushrooms
4 tablespoons olive oil
¼ cup minced onions
1 teaspoon salt
¼ teaspoon freshly ground black pepper
4 tablespoons lemon juice
2 tablespoons brandy
2 tablespoons minced parsley

Wash the mushrooms and drain well. Heat the oil in a skillet; sauté the onions 3 minutes. Add the mushrooms; sauté 2 minutes. Stir in the salt, pepper and lemon juice. Cover and cook over low heat 5 minutes. Stir in the brandy. Chill for 3 hours before serving, sprinkled with the parsley.

SERVES : 4–6 as part of an *antipasto*.

Caponata alla Siciliana

EGGPLANT RELISH SALAD

2 eggplants
2 teaspoons salt
½ cup olive oil
1½ pounds tomatoes, diced
2 stalks celery, diced
½ cup sliced black olives
2 tablespoons capers
1 tablespoon vinegar
1 teaspoon sugar
½ teaspoon freshly ground black pepper

Peel and dice the eggplant and sprinkle with 1 teaspoon salt; let stand 10 minutes. Drain. Heat half the oil in a skillet; brown the eggplant in it.

In a saucepan, heat the remaining oil, mix in the tomatoes and celery; cook over low heat 15 minutes. Add the olives, capers, vinegar, sugar and pepper; cook 15 minutes. Add the browned eggplant and cook 15 minutes longer. Taste for seasoning; chill. Garnish with additional capers and olives, if desired.

SERVES : 6–8

Antipasto di Funghi e Pomodori

MUSHROOM AND TOMATO APPETIZER

4 firm tomatoes
1 teaspoon salt
½ teaspoon freshly ground black pepper
1 teaspoon minced fresh basil or ⅛ teaspoon dried basil
3 tablespoons olive oil
2 tablespoons lemon juice
8 large mushrooms, thinly sliced

Peel and slice the tomatoes. Arrange on a serving dish. Season with the salt, pepper and basil, then sprinkle with half the olive oil and lemon juice. Arrange the sliced mushrooms over them, then sprinkle with the remaining oil and lemon juice.

SERVES : 4–6

Fagioli alla Toscana

TUSCAN-STYLE BEANS

1½ cups dried white beans
¾ cup olive oil
2 cups sliced onions
1½ teaspoons salt
½ teaspoon freshly ground pepper
2 tablespoons minced parsley

Wash the beans, cover with water and bring to a boil. Let soak 1 hour. Drain, cover with fresh water and bring to a boil. Cover and cook over low heat 1½ hours or until tender. Drain.

Heat the oil in a skillet; sauté the onions until light brown.

Remove from the heat and combine with the beans, salt and pepper. Chill. Sprinkle with the parsley and serve cold as an antipasto.

SERVES : 4–6

Fagioli con Caviale

WHITE BEANS AND CAVIAR

2 cups dried white beans
2 teaspoons salt
¼ cup olive oil
¼ teaspoon freshly ground black pepper
½ cup black caviar

Wash the beans, cover with water and bring to a boil; let soak 1 hour. Drain, add fresh water to cover and bring to a boil; cover and cook over low heat 2 hours or until tender. Add the salt after 1 hour of cooking time. Drain and cool.

Toss the beans with the oil and pepper. Mix in the caviar lightly. Serve with lemon wedges.

SERVES : 6–8

Crostini di Fegato

CHICKEN LIVER PÂTÉ ON TOAST

1 pound chicken livers
4 tablespoons butter
¼ cup finely chopped onions
½ cup chicken broth
1 teaspoon salt
¼ teaspoon freshly ground black pepper
2 teaspoons drained capers

Wash the livers, removing any discolored areas and connective tissues. Purée the raw livers in an electric blender or chop very fine.

Melt the butter in a skillet; sauté the onions until yellow and transparent. Add the broth; cook over medium heat 5 minutes. Stir in the livers, salt and pepper until no pink remains; mix constantly. Remove from heat and add the capers. Chill. Spread on sautéed Italian or French bread.

SERVES : 4–6

Crostini di Acciughe

ANCHOVIES ON TOAST

3 cans anchovy fillets
2 tablespoons minced onion
2 cloves garlic, minced
3 tablespoons minced parsley
2 tablespoons olive oil
1 tablespoon lemon juice
Buttered toast rounds

Chop the undrained anchovies to a paste. Mix in the onions, garlic, parsley, olive oil and lemon juice. Spread on the toast and place on a buttered baking pan. Bake in a 475° oven 5 minutes and serve immediately.

MAKES : ABOUT 18

Insalata di Carne Cruda

BEEF TARTAR

1 pound lean trimmed sirloin steak
½ cup lemon juice
6 anchovy fillets, mashed
¼ cup olive oil
½ teaspoon salt
¼ teaspoon freshly ground black pepper
1 teaspoon prepared mustard
¼ cup capers
Pitted black olives

Grind the steak twice just before you start the preparation. Ground sirloin may be bought, but be sure the grinder at the store has not been used for pork. However, the beef will have a better flavor if you grind it yourself.

Mix the ground beef with ⅛ cup lemon juice and let stand in the refrigerator 1 hour. Beat the anchovies and oil until creamy then mix into the meat with the salt, pepper, mustard and remaining lemon juice. Form into four mounds and garnish with the capers and olives. Tiny balls make a delicious hors d'oeuvre.

SERVES : 4, or makes about 36 olive-sized balls for hors d'oeuvres.

Bresaola con Fagioli

SMOKED BEEF AND BEANS

2 cups dried white beans (cannellini, if available)
2 teaspoons salt
½ teaspoon freshly ground black pepper
¼ cup olive oil
2 tablespoons butter
1 cup thinly sliced onions
2 tablespoons tomato paste
1 cup beef broth
1 6-ounce can bresaola (smoked beef), drained

Wash the beans, cover with water, bring to a boil, cook 2 minutes, remove from heat and let soak 1 hour. Drain and add fresh water to cover. Bring to a boil and cook over medium heat 2 hours or until tender. Add the salt and pepper after 1 hour. Drain.

Heat the oil and butter in a skillet; sauté the onions over low heat 15 minutes. Mix in the tomato paste diluted with the broth.

In a casserole, make successive layers of beans, sauce and sliced beef. Cover and bake in a 325° oven 30 minutes. Serve very hot.

SERVES 4–6

Bresaola e Mellone

DRIED BEEF AND MELON

1 6-ounce can bresaola (smoked beef)
1 melon (canteloupe, honey dew, etc.)

Drain the bresaola and separate into slices.
Cut the melon into wedges and remove from the rind. Arrange on plates with 2 slices of bresaola on each.

SERVES : 4–5

Prosciutto e Mellone

HAM AND MELON

Substitute prosciutto for the bresaola.
Note: For an unusual cocktail accompaniment, cut the melon into cubes. Wrap a piece of bresaola or prosciutto around each cube and secure with a cocktail pick.

Bresaola Ripiena

STUFFED DRIED BEEF

1 6-ounce can bresaola (smoked beef)
⅛ pound Gorgonzola or Roquefort cheese
1 3-ounce package cream cheese
¼ cup minced parsley

Drain the bresaola. Cut each slice in half lengthwise. Mash until smooth the Gorgonzola and cream cheese. Spread some on each piece and roll up like a pinwheel. Fasten with a cocktail pick and dip ends lightly in parsley.

MAKES : 18

Bagna Cauda

HOT ANCHOVY DIP

¼ pound butter
¼ cup olive oil
6 cloves garlic, minced
½ cup finely chopped anchovies
1 truffle, sliced thin

Combine butter, olive oil and garlic in the top of a double boiler. Place over hot water, and cook over low heat, stirring constantly until butter melts. Remove from heat, but do not remove the top of the double boiler from the hot water. Add the anchovies and truffle, stirring well. Set aside for 10 minutes and then serve as a dip for crisp raw vegetables.

MAKES : 1 cup

Vitello Tonnato

VEAL WITH TUNA FISH SAUCE

3 pounds rolled leg of veal
1 teaspoon salt
½ teaspoon freshly ground black pepper
½ cup sliced onion
1 carrot, sliced
3 sprigs parsley
1 clove garlic
1 clove
4 cups boiling water
1 7¾-ounce can tuna fish
8 anchovy fillets
¼ cup lemon juice
¾ cup olive oil
2 teaspoons capers

Rub the veal with the salt and ¼ teaspoon pepper. Place in a Dutch oven or heavy saucepan and brown it over high heat. Pour off the fat. Add the onion, carrot, parsley, garlic, clove and boiling water. Cover and cook over low heat 1½ hours or until tender. Drain, dry and cool.

Purée the tuna fish, anchovies, and lemon juice in an electric blender (or mash very smooth). Very gradually beat in the oil, until the consistency of thin mayonnaise. Mix in the capers.

Place the veal in a glass or pottery bowl; pour sauce over it. Marinate in the refrigerator 24 hours before serving. Slice very thin, with the sauce on top.

SERVES : 8–12 as a first course.

Insalata alla Cesare "Romeo"

CAESAR SALAD, ROMEO

4 breadsticks, broken into bite-sized pieces
½ cup olive oil
2 cloves garlic, minced
1 head romaine lettuce, washed and dried
1 teaspoon salt
¼ teaspoon freshly ground black pepper
1 egg
3 tablespoons wine vinegar
6 anchovies, chopped
1 tablespoon capers, chopped
¼ cup grated Romano or Parmesan cheese

Soak the breadsticks in a mixture of ¼ cup oil and the garlic.

Tear the lettuce into a bowl. Season with the salt and pepper; pour the remaining oil over it and toss to coat the lettuce. Break the raw egg into the bowl and toss again. Add the vinegar, anchovies and capers. Toss again. Finally add the cheese and breadsticks. Toss and serve.

SERVES : 2–4

Tortino di Carciofi

ARTICHOKE PIE

3 tablespoons olive oil
1 package frozen artichokes, thawed
2 cans anchovy fillets, drained and cut in half
3 tomatoes, peeled and sliced
1 cup sliced black olives
1 cup fresh bread crumbs

Brush an 8-inch pie plate with a little oil. In it, arrange as many successive layers as possible of the artichokes, anchovies, tomatoes, olives and bread crumbs. Top layer should be bread crumbs. Sprinkle with the remaining oil. Bake in a 350° oven 25 minutes. Cut into wedges.

SERVES : 4–6

Fagioli Toscani col Tonno

BEAN AND TUNA FISH APPETIZER

1½ cups dried white beans
1 clove garlic, split
2 teaspoons salt
½ cup thinly sliced onions
½ cup olive oil
½ teaspoon freshly ground black pepper
2 7¾-ounce cans tuna fish

Wash the beans, cover with water and bring to a boil; let soak 1 hour. Drain, add fresh water to cover and the garlic. Bring to a boil and cook over low heat 2 hours or until tender. Add the salt after 1½ hours cooking time. Drain well, and discard the garlic.

Toss the beans with the onions (separated into rings), the oil and pepper. Chill. Drain the tuna and cut into chunks. Arrange on top of the beans.

SERVES : 6–8

Mozzarella Milanese

FRIED CHEESE STICKS

1 pound mozzarella cheese
½ cup flour
2 eggs, beaten
½ cup dry bread crumbs
1½ cups vegetable oil

Slice the cheese ¼-inch thick, then into sticks 4-inches long by 1-inch wide. Roll in the flour, then dip in the eggs and finally in the bread crumbs, coating them well.

Heat the oil in a skillet until it bubbles. Fry a few sticks at a time until browned. Drain and serve hot.

SERVES : 4–6

Mozzarella in Carrozza

FRIED CHEESE SANDWICHES WITH
ANCHOVY SAUCE

12 slices white bread
6 slices mozzarella cheese
1 cup milk
¾ cup flour
2 eggs, beaten
½ cup olive oil
1 can anchovy fillets, minced
1 tablespoon lemon juice
1 clove garlic, minced (optional)

Trim the crusts off the bread. If you like, cut into rounds or fingers. Cut the cheese to fit the bread. Make 6 sandwiches. Dip in the milk, then the flour, and finally the eggs.

Heat the oil in a skillet until it bubbles and smokes. Brown the sandwiches in it on both sides. Remove and drain. To the oil remaining (if there isn't about ¼ cup, add a little more) add the anchovies, lemon juice and garlic. Cook 30 seconds, and pour over the sandwiches. Serve hot.

SERVES : 6

Spedino alla Romana

MOZZARELLA ON SKEWERS WITH
ANCHOVY SAUCE

1 loaf unsliced white bread
1 cup milk
1 pound mozzarella cheese
¾ cup flour
2 eggs, beaten
3 tablespoons butter
3 tablespoons olive oil

Cut the bread into slices about ¾-inch thick. Trim the crusts. Cut the slices into 1½-inch squares. Soak in the milk 2 minutes; drain. Cut the cheese the same size. Thread the bread and cheese on six skewers, starting and ending with the bread. (Use 5 pieces of bread and 4 of cheese for each skewer.) Start and end with bread, keeping cheese and bread close together. Roll the skewered ingredients in the flour, the eggs, and flour again, coating them well. Heat the butter and oil in a skillet; sauté the *spedino* until browned and crisp on all sides. Slide off the skewers at the table. Prepare the sauce while the skewers are baking.

Sauce:

6 tablespoons butter
½ cup chopped anchovies
2 tablespoons minced parsley

Melt the butter in a skillet; sauté the anchovies and parsley 2 minutes. Pour over the *spedino*.

SERVES : 6

Minestre e Minestrone

SOUPS

To most Americans, the classic soup of Italy is undoubtedly *minestrone*, a very thick vegetable soup containing strands of pasta. The distinction is sometimes drawn in Italy between *minestra* (light soups) and *minestrone* (thick, heavy soups), but this difference is not always agreed upon. It seems clear, however, how *minestra* first originated some fifteen hundred years ago. Italy became a unified country only about a century ago; before that time, there were principalities, dukedoms and small kingdoms, all of which were on good and bad terms, at various times, with one another over the centuries. Inns and hotels were very few in those days of almost continual warfare, and it was only at a monastery that the tired traveler could be assured of obtaining something to eat, for the peasants would lock themselves into their houses at sunset in fear of marauding soldiers. At the monasteries, each morning the good monks would prepare a tremendous pot of thick meat and vegetable soup, which they dispensed to the hungry travelers in the evening, never refusing a single person their generous hospitality. In passing, the very word *minestra* comes from the Latin for "to hand over."

But good soups in Italy do not begin and end with minestrone. There are many superb soups, worthy of anyone's attention. My advice to those who follow these recipes is to prepare a fairly large quantity of soup, using what is required for a particular night's dinner and freezing what is left. Then, in a matter of minutes, frozen soup will be ready once again. One word of caution: if the recipe contains *pasta*, don't add it until you reheat the frozen soup, for *pastas* do not freeze well.

Zuppa alla Pavese

EGG SOUP

4 cups chicken or beef broth
4 eggs
4 slices sautéed Italian or French bread, quartered
Grated Parmesan cheese

In a deep skillet bring the broth to a boil. Break 1 egg at a time into a saucer, then slide it gently into the soup. Cook until set, then skim out and place in a hot soup plate. Continue cooking the remaining eggs. Bring the broth to a boil again, then strain over the eggs. Arrange the bread around the eggs and sprinkle with cheese.

SERVES : 4

Zuppa di Scarola e Fagioli

ESCAROLE AND BEAN SOUP

2 cups dried white beans
8 cups water
2 slices salt pork, chopped
1 cup chopped onions
2 tablespoons flour
2 teaspoons salt
½ teaspoon freshly ground black pepper
1 bunch escarole, shredded

Wash the beans; cover with water, bring to a boil and let soak 1 hour. Drain, and add the 8 cups water. Bring to a boil, cover and cook over low heat 1½ hours.

In a skillet, cook the salt pork and onions until browned. Blend in the flour. Add to the beans with the salt and pepper. Cook 30 minutes. Add the escarole; cook 30 minutes longer or until beans are tender. Taste for seasoning.

SERVES : 6

Soffioncini in Brodo

LIGHT DUMPLINGS IN SOUP

3 tablespoons butter
4 tablespoons flour
½ teaspoon salt
2 cups milk
1 egg and 1 extra egg yolk
1 cup grated Parmesan cheese
2 tablespoons minced parsley
8 cups beef or chicken broth

Melt the butter in a saucepan; blend in the flour and salt. Gradually add the milk, stirring steadily to the boiling point, then cook over low heat 10 minutes, stirring occasionally. Cool. Beat in the egg, egg yolk, cheese and parsley. Shape into walnut-sized balls.

Bring the broth to a boil; drop the dumplings into it. Cover and cook over low heat 5 minutes or until dumplings rise to the surface.

SERVES : 8

Stracciatella alla Romana

EGG-RIBBON SOUP

3 eggs
1 tablespoon cold water
¼ cup freshly grated Romano or Parmesan cheese
2 tablespoons minced parsley
6 cups chicken broth

Beat the eggs and water in a bowl; stir in the cheese and parsley. Just before serving, bring the broth to a boil. Slowly pour the egg mixture into the soup, stirring steadily with a fork until eggs set. Serve immediately.

SERVES : 6–8

Zuppa di Spinaci e Uova

SPINACH–EGG SOUP

2 pounds spinach or 2 packages, frozen
4 tablespoons butter
1¼ teaspoons salt
¼ teaspoon white pepper
⅛ teaspoon nutmeg
4 egg yolks
¼ cup grated Parmesan cheese
6 cups boiling chicken broth

Cook the spinach 4 minutes. Drain thoroughly. Purée in an electric blender or force through a sieve.

Melt the butter in a saucepan; add the spinach, salt, pepper and nutmeg. Cook over low heat 2 minutes, stirring almost constantly. Beat the egg yolks and cheese; mix into the spinach. Gradually add the broth, stirring constantly. Bring to a boil (the eggs will curdle, so don't worry) and serve with croutons.

SERVES : 8

Brodo

CONSOMMÉ

8 cups beef broth
½ pound ground beef
2 egg whites

Bring the broth to a boil. Add the meat in small pieces. Cook over low heat 1 hour. Stir the egg whites and egg shells into the soup (to clarify), then strain through a very fine sieve or cheesecloth.

SERVES : 6–8

Pallottoline Deliziose

CHEESE DUMPLINGS IN BEEF BROTH

1¼ cups grated Gruyère or Swiss cheese
1 cup sifted flour
⅛ teaspoon salt
1 egg, beaten
1 tablespoon melted butter
¾ cup dry bread crumbs
¼ cup olive oil
8 cups beef broth

Knead the cheese, flour and salt together. Mix in the egg and melted butter, kneading until a ball of dough is formed. If too dry, add a teaspoon of milk. Shape teaspoons of the mixture into balls and roll in the bread crumbs. Heat the oil until it sizzles, then fry the balls until browned on all sides. Shake the skillet frequently to turn balls. Drain and cool.

Bring the broth to a boil and drop the cheese balls into it. Cook over low heat 5 minutes.

SERVES : 8

Minestrina Fine

BEEF BROTH WITH PASTINA

6 cups beef broth
3 tablespoons minute tapioca
¾ cup pastina
Grated Parmesan cheese

Bring the broth to a boil; stir in the tapioca. Cook over low heat 10 minutes. Mix in the pastina; cook 5 minutes longer. Serve with the grated cheese.

SERVES : 6

Zuppa all'Ortolana

ITALIAN VEGETABLE SOUP

1 cup chick peas
3 tablespoons olive oil
¾ cup chopped onions
2 cloves garlic, minced
¼ cup chopped celery
½ cup diced carrots
1½ cups diced zucchini
1 cup diced potatoes
1½ cups coarsely chopped cabbage
2 tablespoons tomato paste
8 cups boiling water
2 teaspoons salt
½ teaspoon freshly ground black pepper
¼ teaspoon basil
2 tablespoons minced parsley
1 cup cooked macaroni

Wash the chick peas, cover with water and bring to a boil. Let soak 1 hour. Drain, add fresh water to cover and cook over medium heat 1½ hours. Drain. (Use 2 cups canned chick peas if you prefer.)

Heat the oil in a saucepan; sauté the onions, garlic and celery 5 minutes. Mix in the carrots, zucchini, potatoes and cabbage; cook 5 minutes. Stir in the tomato paste, then add the water, chick peas, salt, pepper and basil. Bring to a boil, cover and cook over low heat 1 hour. Mix in the parsley and macaroni; cook 5 minutes and taste for seasoning. Serve with grated Parmesan cheese.

SERVES : 6–8

Minestrone alla Genovese

VEGETABLE SOUP, GENOA STYLE

2 tablespoons olive oil
1 cup grated carrots
1 cup chopped onions
2 leeks, sliced
2 cups peeled diced potatoes
2 cups shredded spinach
2 quarts water
3 cups cooked or canned kidney beans
2 teaspoons salt
½ teaspoon freshly ground black pepper
3 tablespoons minced parsley
¼ teaspoon basil
2 cloves garlic, minced
4 slices bacon, diced
1½ cups macaroni

Heat the oil in a saucepan; cook the carrots, onions, leeks, potatoes and spinach in it 5 minutes. Add the water, beans, salt and pepper; bring to a boil and cook over low heat 1 hour. In an electric blender, purée the parsley, basil, garlic and bacon, or pound ingredients to a paste with a mortar and pestle. Add to the soup with the macaroni. Cook 20 minutes or until macaroni is tender. Serve with grated Pecorino or Parmesan cheese.

SERVES : 6–8

Minestrone alla Milanese

VEGETABLE SOUP, MILAN STYLE

1 cup dried white beans
2½ quarts water
3 slices bacon, diced
2 tablespoons olive oil
1 cup thinly sliced onions
1 carrot, diced
1 cup diced potatoes
2 cups diced zucchini
1 cup peeled diced tomatoes
3 cups shredded cabbage
1 tablespoon salt
½ teaspoon freshly ground black pepper
1 clove garlic, minced
½ teaspoon basil
¼ cup raw rice
3 tablespoons minced parsley
½ cup grated Parmesan cheese

Wash the beans, cover with water and bring to a boil. Let soak 1 hour, drain and add the 2½ quarts water. Bring to a boil and cook over low heat 1½ hours. Meanwhile, prepare the vegetables.

In a skillet, lightly brown the bacon. Pour off the fat. Add the oil and onions. Sauté 5 minutes. Mix in the carrot, potatoes and zucchini; sauté 5 minutes, stirring frequently. Add to the beans (after they have cooked 1½ hours) with the tomatoes, cabbage, salt, pepper, garlic and basil. Cook over low heat 1¼ hours. Mix in the rice and parsley; cook 20 minutes longer. Just before serving, stir in the cheese. Serve with additional grated cheese.

SERVES : 8–10

Zuppa di Broccoli

BROCCOLI AND MACARONI SOUP

⅛ pound salt pork, chopped fine
1 tablespoon olive oil
1 clove garlic, minced
3 tablespoons tomato paste
6 cups water
1 teaspoon salt
¼ teaspoon black pepper
3 cups broccoli flowerets or 1 package frozen broccoli
    flowerets
2 cups short macaroni
⅓ cup grated Parmesan cheese

Brown the salt pork in a saucepan; add the oil, garlic, to-mato paste, water, salt and pepper; bring to a boil and cook over low heat 20 minutes. Add the broccoli, cover and cook 5 minutes. Mix in the macaroni and cook 10 minutes longer. Serve with the cheese.

SERVES : 4–5

Noccioline di Vitello in Brodo

MEAT BALL SOUP

½ pound ground veal
1 egg
2 tablespoons grated Parmesan cheese
2 tablespoons bread crumbs
½ teaspoon salt
⅛ teaspoon freshly ground black pepper
8 cups chicken or beef broth

Mix together thoroughly the veal, egg, cheese, bread crumbs, salt and pepper. Form into walnut-sized balls.

Bring the broth to a boil; drop the meat balls into it. Cook over low heat 20 minutes. Serve with grated Parmesan cheese.

SERVES : 6–8

Zuppa di Piselli

SPLIT PEA SOUP, LOMBARDY STYLE

2 cups split peas
2½ quarts water
¼ cup olive oil
½ cup grated carrots
1 cup chopped onions
1 clove garlic, minced
½ cup diced celery
¼ cup chopped parsley
2 teaspoons salt
½ teaspoon freshly ground black pepper
1 bay leaf
1 cup milk

Wash the split peas and soak in warm water 1 hour. Drain; add the 2½ quarts water. Bring to a boil and cook over low heat 2½ hours.

Heat the oil in a skillet; sauté the carrots, onions, garlic and celery 10 minutes. Add to the soup with the parsley, salt, pepper and bay leaf. Cook 30 minutes longer. Discard bay leaf; purée the mixture in an electric blender or force through a sieve. Return to saucepan and stir in the milk. Heat and serve.

SERVES : 6–8

Minestra di Ceci alla Milanese

CHICK PEA SOUP, MILANESE STYLE

1 pound dried chick peas
3 quarts water
2 tablespoons olive oil
1 slice bacon, diced
1 cup chopped onions
¼ pound mushrooms, sliced
2 Italian sausages, sliced
2½ teaspoons salt
½ teaspoon black pepper

¼ teaspoon sage
2 tomatoes, peeled and chopped

Wash the chick peas, cover with water and bring to a boil; let soak 1 hour. Drain. Add the 3 quarts water. Bring to a boil and cook over low heat 2½ hours. Remove about 1 cup beans; purée in an electric blender or force through a sieve. Return to the saucepan.

Cook the oil and bacon in a skillet 2 minutes. Add the onions and mushrooms and sauté 10 minutes. Brown the sausages and drain. Add vegetables and sausages to the soup with the salt, pepper, sage and tomatoes. Cook 30 minutes longer. Taste for seasoning. Serve with grated cheese.

SERVES : 8–10

Zuppa di Fagioli

BEAN SOUP

2 cups dried white beans
2½ quarts water
Beef bone
2½ teaspoons salt
½ teaspoon white pepper
2 tablespoons olive oil
¾ cup finely chopped onions
1 clove garlic, minced
3 tablespoons minced parsley

Wash the beans, cover with water, bring to a boil and let soak 1 hour. Drain. Add the 2½ quarts water and the bone. Bring to a boil and cook over low heat 2½ hours, adding the salt and pepper after 1 hour. Discard the bone. Purée half the beans in an electric blender or force through a sieve. Return to saucepan.

Heat the oil in a skillet; sauté the onions 10 minutes. Stir in the garlic; cook 1 minute. Add to the soup; cook 20 minutes longer. Taste for seasoning. Stir in the parsley just before serving.

SERVES : 6–8

Pasta e Fagioli "Monelli"

MACARONI AND BEAN SOUP

2 cups dried white beans
1 beef bone
3 quarts water
¼ cup olive oil
2 cloves garlic, minced
½ teaspoon rosemary
1 tablespoon flour
2 teaspoons tomato paste
1 cup beef broth
2 teaspoons salt
½ teaspoon freshly ground black pepper
2 tablespoons minced parsley
1 cup macaroni, broken into small pieces

Wash the beans, cover with water, bring to a boil and let soak 1 hour. Drain. Add the bone and the 3 quarts water. Bring to a boil, cover loosely and cook over low heat 2 hours.

Heat the oil in a saucepan; sauté the garlic 1 minute. Blend in the rosemary, flour and tomato paste, then stir in the broth, salt and pepper. Cook, stirring steadily, until mixture boils. Add to the beans. Cook 1 hour longer. If too thick, add a little boiling water. Mix in the parsley and macaroni. Cook 10 minutes longer, or until macaroni is tender. This is an extremely thick soup.

SERVES : 6–8

Minestra Genovese di Fagiolini al Pesto

BEAN SOUP, GENOA STYLE

2 cups dried navy beans
2½ quarts water
1½ cups peeled diced potatoes

1 stalk celery, diced
1 leek, thinly sliced
1 cup grated carrots
1½ teaspoons salt
½ teaspoon freshly ground black pepper
2 slices bacon, diced
1 clove garlic, minced
2 tablespoons minced parsley
½ teaspoon basil
1 tablespoon olive oil
2 tablespoons grated Parmesan cheese
1 cup uncooked broad noodles

Wash the beans. Cover with water and bring to a boil. Let soak 1 hour. Drain; add the 2½ quarts water, bring to a boil and cook over low heat 2½ hours. Add the potatoes, celery, leek, carrots, salt and pepper; cook 30 minutes.

In an electric blender, purée the bacon, garlic, parsley, basil, olive oil and cheese (rinse bowl with a little soup) or pound ingredients together to a paste with a mortar and pestle. Add to the soup; cook 10 minutes. Mix in the noodles; cook 10 minutes longer.

SERVES : 6–8

Minestrone di Riso alla Milanese

RICE SOUP, MILANESE STYLE

1 cup dried kidney beans
1 tablespoon olive oil
1 slice bacon, diced
¾ cup chopped celery
¾ cup chopped onions
¾ cup grated carrots
1½ cups peeled diced potatoes
1 cup peeled diced tomatoes
1½ teaspoons salt

½ teaspoon freshly ground black pepper
½ teaspoon basil
8 cups beef broth
2 cups shredded cabbage
¾ cup raw rice
3 tablespoons minced parsley
2 tablespoons butter
½ cup grated Parmesan cheese

Wash the beans, cover with water and bring to a boil. Let soak 1 hour; drain, add fresh water to cover, bring to a boil and cook over low heat 2 hours. Drain.

In a large saucepan, cook the oil and bacon until bacon browns. Mix in the celery, onions, carrots, potatoes, tomatoes, salt, pepper and basil; cook 5 minutes. Add the broth, cabbage and beans; bring to a boil and cook over low heat 20 minutes. Stir in the rice; cook 20 minutes. Stir in the parsley, butter and cheese. Remove from heat and let stand 5 minutes before serving. This is an extremely thick, filling soup.

SERVES : 8–10

Minestra Piemontese

RICE SOUP, PIEDMONT STYLE

7 cups chicken or beef broth
1 stalk celery, diced
2 leeks, sliced
1 carrot, grated
1 cup raw washed rice
2 egg yolks
2 tablespoons minced parsley
2 tablespoons cold water
1 cup grated Parmesan cheese

Cook the broth, celery, leeks and carrot 20 minutes; stir in the rice. Cook over medium heat 20 minutes. Taste for seasoning.

Beat the egg yolks, parsley, water and cheese in a tureen or bowl. Gradually add the soup, stirring constantly.

SERVES : 6–8

Zuppa alla Cacciatora

HUNTER'S SOUP

2 dried mushrooms
2 tablespoons butter
¾ cup chopped onions
1 pound ground veal
2 quarts beef broth
¼ teaspoon freshly ground black pepper
3 egg yolks
½ cup light cream

Wash the mushrooms, cover with water and let soak 15 minutes. Drain and chop. Melt the butter in a saucepan; sauté the onions 5 minutes. Mix in the veal; cook over medium heat 10 minutes, stirring frequently. Add the broth, pepper and mushrooms; cook over low heat 1½ hours. Force the mixture through a sieve. Taste for seasoning. Just before serving, bring the soup to a boil. Beat the egg yolks and cream in a tureen or bowl; gradually add the soup, stirring steadily to prevent curdling. Serve immediately with croutons.

SERVES : 6–8

Zuppa di Asparagi

CREAM OF ASPARAGUS SOUP

2 pounds asparagus or 2 packages frozen, thawed
   asparagus
3 cups sliced potatoes

1 cup sliced leeks
½ cup sliced onions
2 quarts water
2 teaspoons salt
¼ teaspoon white pepper
1 egg yolk
1 cup heavy cream

Wash the fresh asparagus, cut away the tough white part and discard. Cut off twelve–fourteen 1½-inch pieces from the tip ends of fresh asparagus and reserve. Or cut off twelve–fourteen 1½-inch tips from the frozen asparagus and reserve. Slice the remaining fresh or frozen asparagus in 1-inch pieces. Combine in a saucepan with the potatoes, leeks, onions, water, salt and pepper. Bring to a boil and cook over low heat 35 minutes. Purée in an electric blender, then strain, or force through a sieve.

Return to the saucepan and add the reserved tips and butter. Cook over low heat 10 minutes.

Beat the egg yolk and cream in a bowl; add a little of the hot soup, stirring steadily to prevent curdling. Return to balance of the soup. Heat, but do not let boil. Serve with a couple of tips in each plate, and with croutons.

SERVES : 6–8

Zuppa di Pomodori

TOMATO SOUP

2 pounds tomatoes, peeled and diced
½ cup sliced onions
1¼ teaspoons salt
⅛ teaspoon white pepper
1 tablespoon butter
1 tablespoon flour
1 cup milk

Cook the tomatoes, onions, salt and pepper over very low heat for 30 minutes, stirring frequently. Purée in an electric blender or force through a sieve. Return to a clean saucepan.

Melt the butter in a saucepan; blend in the flour. Add the milk, stirring steadily to the boiling point. Mix into the tomatoes; cook 10 minutes. Taste for seasoning and serve with croutons.

SERVES : 6–8

Brodetto alla Marinara

FISH BROTH, SAILOR'S STYLE

2 pounds assorted fish
1 16-ounce can tomatoes
¼ cup olive oil
1 clove garlic, minced
1 onion, sliced
2 tablespoons white vinegar
1½ cups water
½ cup dry white wine
1½ teaspoons salt
¼ teaspoon freshly ground black pepper
2 tablespoons minced parsley

You may buy any kind of fish, as the fish itself is not served. Ask for a small fish head, too. Wash the fish.

Mash the tomatoes very fine. In a saucepan, heat the oil. Sauté the garlic and onion 5 minutes. Add the vinegar; cover and cook over low heat 5 minutes. Mix in the tomatoes, water, wine, salt, pepper and fish. Bring to a boil and cook over low heat 45 minutes. Strain, pressing through firmly; be sure bones and skin do not go through. Reheat, taste for seasoning, and stir in the parsley. Serve with sautéed Italian bread.

SERVES : 4–5

Pesce

FISH

Italy is a country with a very long coastline, and the variety and selection of fish sometimes appears limitless. On the west coast, the region from Genoa down to Naples, the fish are of the Mediterranean type, full of a strong sea-flavor. On the east coast, from Venice down to Bari, Italy fronts on the Adriatic and it is from this extraordinary body of water that some of the most delicate fish and shellfish in the world may be found.

From the Adriatic come *scampi,* a type of shrimp or prawn. *Scampi* are actually a distinct and separate variety of shellfish, although by some error, it has come to mean broiled shrimp prepared in garlic and olive oil. This misnomer persists, but the fact remains that *scampi* are undoubtedly the finest variety of shrimp or prawn in the world. Although American shrimp are excellent, *scampi* are absolutely incomparable and for this reason, I import *scampi* to serve in my restaurant.

Italian fish dishes are somewhat unusual to most Americans, accustomed to eating merely broiled or fried fish. Sauces are particularly important in these Italian preparations, shellfish

38

often being combined with fish. Even those Americans who regard themselves as solely meat-eaters will find interesting fish dishes in this section.

Filetti di Sogliole Spumanti

FILLET OF SOLE IN WHITE WINE

4 fillets of sole
1¼ teaspoons salt
½ teaspoon white pepper
2 green onions, chopped
¼ cup melted butter
½ cup dry white wine
1 tablespoon chopped parsley
½ teaspoon thyme
2 bay leaves, crushed
1 tablespoon butter
1½ teaspoons flour
2 tablespoons heavy cream

Wash and dry the fillets; season with the salt and pepper. Arrange fillets in buttered baking dish in single layer and sprinkle with the green onions, melted butter, wine, parsley, thyme and bay leaves. Cover with greased paper facing down, then cover dish and bake in a 375° oven 20 minutes. Carefully remove fillets from baking dish. Strain pan juices into a small saucepan, add butter and let melt. Blend in flour, add cream and cook 4 minutes. Pour over fish and serve.

SERVES : 4

Sogliole al Vino Rosso

FILLET OF SOLE IN RED WINE

4 fillets of sole
Fish trimmings
2½ teaspoons salt
½ teaspoon freshly ground black pepper
1½ cups dry red wine
2 cups water
¼ cup sliced mushrooms
1 onion
2 cloves
1 carrot
1 stalk celery
1 clove garlic, split
¼ teaspoon thyme
1 bay leaf
4 tablespoons butter
2 tablespoons flour
2 teaspoons anchovy paste
2 teaspoons lemon juice

Wash and dry the fillets. Wash the fish trimmings. (When buying the fillets ask for a small fish head and some skin and bones.) Season the fillets with 1½ teaspoons salt and ¼ teaspoon pepper.

In a saucepan, combine the wine, water, mushrooms, onion stuck with cloves, carrot, celery, garlic, thyme, bay leaf, fish trimmings and the remaining salt and pepper. Bring to a boil and cook over low heat 45 minutes. Strain through a fine sieve.

Melt 2 tablespoons butter in a baking dish. Arrange the fillets in it and add ¼ cup of the stock. Bake in a 325° oven 25 minutes or until fish flakes easily when tested with a fork.

While the fish is baking, knead the flour with the remaining butter. Add to the remaining stock; cook over low heat, stirring constantly until thickened. Mix in the anchovy paste and lemon juice. Taste for seasoning. Pour over the fillets.

SERVES : 4

Sogliole alla Parmigiana

FILLET OF SOLE WITH PARMESAN CHEESE

4 fillets of sole
2 teaspoons salt
½ teaspoon freshly ground black pepper
6 tablespoons butter
¼ cup grated Parmesan cheese
¼ cup bottled clam juice

Wash and dry the fillets. Season with the salt and pepper. Melt 4 tablespoons butter in a skillet; sauté the fish until browned on both sides. Sprinkle with the cheese, dot with the remaining butter and add the clam juice. Cover and cook over low heat 5 minutes.

SERVES : 4

Sogliole in Bianco e Verde

FILLET OF SOLE IN GREEN SAUCE

4 fillets of sole
1½ teaspoons salt
¼ teaspoon white pepper
2 tablespoons olive oil
½ cup dry white wine
½ cup chopped parsley
2 tablespoons heavy cream
½ cup cooked diced shrimp

Wash and dry the fillets; season with the salt and pepper. Heat the oil in a skillet. Arrange the sole in it and add the wine. Bring to a boil and cook over low heat 10 minutes. Add the parsley and cook 10 minutes longer or until fish flakes when tested with a fork. Mix in the cream and shrimp. Heat and serve.

SERVES : 4

Pesce all'Aglio

FISH WITH GARLIC SAUCE

4 fillets of sole
¾ cup flour
1½ teaspoons salt
½ teaspoon black pepper
½ cup vegetable oil
3 cloves garlic, minced
⅛ cup dry bread crumbs
½ cup olive oil
2 tablespoons wine vinegar

Dip the fish in a mixture of the flour, salt and pepper. Heat
the vegetable oil in a skillet; cook the fish in it until browned, and
flakes easily when tested with a fork. Transfer to a heated serving dish. Prepare the sauce while the fish is frying.

Mix the garlic and bread crumbs. Gradually mix in the olive
oil (add enough to make the sauce the consistency of mayonnaise), then the vinegar. Spread over the fish and serve.

SERVES : 4

Sogliole in Aceto

MARINATED FILLET OF SOLE

4 fillets of sole, cut in finger-length pieces
1 teaspoon dry mustard
½ teaspoon black pepper
10 anchovy fillets, chopped
1 tablespoon chopped parsley
½ teaspoon oregano
3 tablespoons olive oil
2 tablespoons lemon juice
1 cup flour
1 egg, lightly beaten

1 cup vegetable oil
Lemon wedges

Wash and dry the fish. Mix together the mustard, pepper, anchovies, parsley, oregano, olive oil and lemon juice; marinate the fish at room temperature in the mixture 1 hour. Remove from marinade; roll in the flour, and dip into the egg. Heat the vegetable oil in a skillet until it bubbles. Fry the sole in it until browned on both sides. Garnish with the lemon wedges.

SERVES : 4

Tonno alla Maniera dei Liguri

TUNA IN SPICY SAUCE

3 dried mushrooms
1 2-pound fresh tuna steak, cut 1-inch thick
2 tablespoons olive oil
2 anchovy fillets, chopped
1 clove garlic, minced
2 tablespoons flour
2 cups dry white wine
1½ teaspoons salt
½ teaspoon freshly ground black pepper
2 tablespoons minced parsley
1 tablespoon lemon juice

Wash the mushrooms; soak in water to cover 10 minutes, drain and chop. Wash and dry the fish.

Heat the oil in a skillet; mix in the anchovies, garlic and mushrooms for 2 minutes. Sprinkle with the flour. Add the wine; bring to a boil and cook over high heat 5 minutes. Add the fish, salt and pepper; cover and cook over low heat 1 hour. Taste for seasoning. Serve sprinkled with the parsley and lemon juice.

SERVES : 4–6

Spigola Marinara

STRIPED BASS IN TOMATO SAUCE

3–4-pound striped bass
2½ teaspoons salt
¾ teaspoon freshly ground black pepper
¼ cup olive oil
4 whole cloves garlic
2 pounds tomatoes, peeled and chopped or 1 29-ounce can,
    chopped
½ teaspoon oregano
½ teaspoon basil

Have the fish cleaned but left whole. The head may be removed or not, as you prefer. Rub the fish with half the salt and pepper. Place in a greased baking pan.

Heat the oil in a saucepan; brown the garlic in it, then discard. Add the tomatoes, oregano, basil and remaining salt and pepper. Bring to a boil and cook over low heat 10 minutes. Pour over the fish; bake in a 425° oven 35 minutes, or until fish flakes easily when tested with a fork. Baste frequently.

SERVES : 3–4

Spigola alla Romana

STRIPED BASS WITH MUSHROOM-
WINE SAUCE

3-pound striped bass
2 teaspoons salt
½ teaspoon freshly ground black pepper
4 tablespoons butter
¾ cup chopped onions
1 clove garlic, minced
6 anchovy fillets, chopped

2 cups dry white wine
½ cup water
2 tablespoons olive oil
½ pound mushrooms, sliced
1 tablespoon flour
2 tablespoons minced parsley

Wash and dry the fish; rub with the salt and pepper.

In a deep large skillet, melt the butter; sauté the onions 5 min-utes. Mix in the garlic and anchovies for 1 minute. Add the wine and water. Bring to a boil and cook over low heat 5 minutes. Place the fish in the skillet; cover loosely and cook over low heat 40 minutes or until fish flakes easily when tested with a fork. Carefully transfer fish to a heated serving dish and keep warm. Reserve stock.

While the fish is cooking, prepare the mushrooms. Heat the oil in a saucepan; sauté the mushrooms 5 minutes. Sprinkle with the flour. Add the fish stock, stirring steadily to the boiling point. Mix in the parsley; cook over low heat 5 minutes. Pour over the fish.

SERVES : 4–6

Spigola alla Livornese

STRIPED BASS IN OLIVE SAUCE

6 slices sea bass (3 pounds)
½ cup flour
2½ teaspoons freshly ground black pepper
½ cup olive oil
2 cloves garlic, minced
2 pounds tomatoes, chopped or 1 29-ounce can tomatoes, drained
1 cup sliced black olives
3 tablespoons minced parsley

Wash and dry the fish. Dip in a mixture of the flour, 1½ teaspoons salt and ¼ teaspoon pepper.

Heat half the oil in a saucepan; sauté the garlic 2 minutes. Add the tomatoes and the remaining salt and pepper; cook over low heat 30 minutes. While the sauce is cooking, heat the remaining oil in a skillet; brown the fish in it. Add to the sauce and cook 15 minutes. Add the olives; cook 5 minutes. Sprinkle with parsley.

SERVES : 6

Pesce alla Pescatora

FISH, FISHERMAN'S STYLE

3 pounds pike, sea bass, etc., sliced
1½ teaspoons salt
½ teaspoon black pepper
2 tablespoons olive oil
1 cup chopped onions
1 clove garlic, minced
½ teaspoon basil
1 carrot, diced
2 tablespoons chopped parsley
3 cups dry red wine
1 tablespoon flour
¼ cup butter

Wash and dry the fish.

Mix together, in a bowl, the salt, pepper, oil, onions, garlic, basil, carrot, parsley and wine. Marinate the fish in the mixture 2 hours. Transfer fish and marinade to large skillet and cook 25 minutes, turning fish once. Remove fish from stock; strain stock and cook 5 minutes longer. Rub together the flour and butter and add to the stock in small pieces, stirring constantly. Return fish to skillet and let stock coat it. Serve hot.

SERVES : 4–6

Sgombro in Salsa di Pomodori

MACKEREL IN TOMATO SAUCE

4 fillets of mackerel
2 tablespoons olive oil
1 cup sliced onions
1 clove garlic, minced
1 tablespoon chopped parsley
1 16-ounce can tomatoes
2 tablespoons water
1 teaspoon salt
½ teaspoon pepper
¼ teaspoon oregano

Wash and dry the fish.

Heat the olive oil in a skillet; sauté the onions, garlic and parsley 5 minutes. Add the tomatoes, water, salt, pepper and oregano; cook 5 minutes. Arrange the fish in the skillet, cover and cook 10 minutes. Turn fish over and cook 10 minutes longer. Serve hot or cold.

SERVES : 4

Pesce Ripieno

STUFFED FISH

5–6-pound fish (bass, whitefish, snapper)
2½ teaspoons salt
¾ teaspoon black pepper
2 cloves garlic, minced
3 tablespoons olive oil
2 cups fresh bread crumbs
3 slices bacon
½ cup chopped green or yellow onions
½ cup chopped celery

½ cup chopped parsley
⅛ teaspoon crushed dried red peppers
2 tablespoons butter
¾ cup dry white wine

Have the fish split and boned for stuffing, and the head and tail removed, if you like. Wash and dry the fish. Rub inside and out with the salt, pepper, garlic and olive oil.

Soak the bread crumbs in water; drain.

Brown the bacon, remove from pan and crumble. Pour off all but 2 tablespoons fat from the pan. In it, sauté the onions and celery 10 minutes. Mix in the parsley, red peppers, soaked bread crumbs and bacon. Stuff the fish and sew or fasten with skewers. Melt the butter in a baking pan. Place the fish in it. Bake in a 400° oven 25 minutes. Add the wine. Reduce heat to 350° and bake 40 minutes longer or until fish flakes easily when tested with a fork.

SERVES : 6–8

Cacciucco

LEGHORN FISH STEW

3 pounds assorted salt-water fish
12 clams
½ cup olive oil
¾ cup chopped onions
2 cloves garlic, minced
1 cup dry red wine
1 20-ounce can tomatoes, drained
1½ teaspoons salt
½ teaspoon crushed dried red peppers
2 tablespoons minced parsley

Be sure the fish you buy is salt-water fish and buy a few kinds, in slices. Wash and dry it. Scrub the clams under cold running water.

Heat the oil in a saucepan; sauté the onions and garlic 5 minutes. Add the wine; cook until reduced to half. Mix in the tomatoes, salt and red peppers. Arrange the fish (not the clams) in it. Bring to a boil and cook over low heat 25 minutes. Add the clams and parsley; cover and cook 5 minutes longer, or until clams open. Serve in deep plates with garlic toast.

SERVES : 6–8

Zuppa di Pesce

FISH STEW

3 pounds assorted sliced fish
⅓ cup olive oil
1½ teaspoons salt
½ teaspoon black pepper
½ teaspoon crushed bay leaf
1 cup chopped onions
1 clove garlic, minced
2 tablespoons tomato paste
1 cup dry white wine
2 cups boiling water

Buy as many varieties of fish as possible—mackerel, bass, sole and eel, to mention some possibilities. Cut fish into 3-inch pieces. Wash and dry.

Heat the oil in a casserole; brown the fish in it lightly. Season with the salt, pepper and bay leaf; cook over low heat 15 minutes, turning the pieces once. Remove the fish carefully and keep warm. In the oil remaining, sauté the onions 10 minutes. Mix in the garlic, tomato paste and wine, then the boiling water. Cook over low heat 25 minutes. Return the fish and cook 10 minutes longer. Taste for seasoning. Serve in deep plates with sautéed bread, rubbed with garlic.

SERVES : 6–8

Agoni Marinati al Forno

BAKED TROUT

4 brook trout
1 cup flour
2 teaspoons salt
½ teaspoon freshly ground black pepper
¼ cup vegetable oil
½ cup cider vinegar
1 carrot, quartered
1 stalk celery
2 cloves garlic
¼ teaspoon marjoram
1 bay leaf
3 sprigs parsley
¼ cup dry bread crumbs
3 tablespoons butter

Wash the trout, and remove the heads, if you like. Dry the fish thoroughly. Dip the fish in a mixture of the flour, salt and pepper. Heat the oil until it sizzles; fry the trout in it until browned on both sides. Drain.

Cook the vinegar, carrot, celery, garlic, marjoram, bay leaf and parsley 15 minutes. Strain. Pour the liquid into a shallow baking pan large enough to hold the trout. Arrange the fish in it. Sprinkle with the bread crumbs. Dot with the butter. Bake in a 400° oven 10 minutes or until bread crumbs brown. Serve hot or cold.

SERVES : 4

Fritto Misto

MIXED FRIED FOODS

Ingredients used in a Fritto Misto can be anything you like, such as fish, fish and vegetables, parboiled sweetbreads and brains, chicken or calf's liver, breast of chicken, scallopine of veal, sliced eggplant, sliced zucchini, sliced artichokes, mushrooms, cauliflower flowerets, green beans. Cut selected foods in bite-sized pieces and sprinkle with salt and pepper before dipping in the batter.

Batter:

2 cups sifted flour
¾ teaspoon salt
¼ teaspoon white pepper
⅛ cup oil
1½ cups lukewarm water
3 egg whites, beaten stiff
Vegetable oil for deep frying

Sift the flour, salt, and pepper into a bowl. Mix in the oil, then gradually beat in the water until it is the consistency of heavy cream. Let stand 2 hours. When ready to use, fold in the egg whites. Dip the selected ingredients in the batter.

Heat the oil to 370°. Fry a few pieces at a time until browned. Drain and keep warm while preparing the balance. Serve sprinkled with parsley and surrounded with lemon wedges.

Makes enough batter to SERVE : 6–8

Baccalá con Olive

SALT COD WITH OLIVES

2 pounds dried cod fish
1 onion
1 tablespoon vinegar
1 cup sliced black olives
4 anchovy fillets, chopped
2 cloves garlic, minced

½ cup capers
¼ cup olive oil
2 tablespoons lemon juice
3 tablespoons minced parsley

Wash the cod fish and soak in cold water to cover over-night. Drain. Add fresh water, the onion and vinegar. Bring to a boil and cook over low heat 1½ hours, or until tender. Drain, cool, and remove skin and bones. Flake the fish.

In a bowl, combine the fish, olives, anchovies, garlic and capers. Toss lightly. Mix together the oil, lemon juice and parsley. Pour over the mixture. Marinate in the refrigerator several hours before serving.

SERVES : 4–6

Calamari in Cassuola

SQUID IN SPICED TOMATO BROTH

1½ pounds very small squid
½ cup olive oil
1 clove garlic
1 cup Tomato Sauce (see recipe, p. 168)
½ cup dry white wine
1 teaspoon salt
⅛ teaspoon dried ground red peppers

Have the fish man skin the squid and clean them for you. Wash thoroughly.

Heat the oil in a deep large skillet; brown the garlic in it and discard. Add the squid; cook over medium heat 10 minutes. Add the Tomato Sauce, wine, salt and red peppers. Cover and cook over low heat 15 minutes.

SERVES : 4–6

Vongole in Bianco alla Marinara

CLAMS IN WHITE SAUCE

36 small hard shell clams
1¼ cups dry white wine
¼ teaspoon thyme
¼ teaspoon crumbled bay leaf
1 tablespoon flour
1 tablespoon butter
3 tablespoons minced parsley

Scrub the clams under cold running water. Combine the clams in a saucepan with the wine, thyme and bay leaf. Cook over high heat until clams open. Remove the clams and keep hot. Discard half the shells, if you like. Strain the stock into a small saucepan. Knead the flour and butter together and add to the stock in small pieces, stirring constantly over medium heat until thickened. Mix in the parsley; add clams and heat 1 minute. Serve clams and sauce in deep plates.

SERVES : 4

Note: Cozze (mussels) may be prepared in the same way.

Zuppa di Vongole

CLAM SOUP

36 small hard-shell clams
4 tablespoons olive oil
1 clove garlic
1 pound tomatoes, chopped or 1 16-ounce can, drained
1 teaspoon salt
½ cup dry white wine
2 tablespoons chopped parsley
4 slices Italian bread, toasted

Scrub the clams under cold running water. Put in a skillet, cover and cook over low heat until clams open. Remove the clams from the shells and strain any pan juices.

Heat the oil in a saucepan. Add the garlic and remove when brown. Add the tomatoes, salt and wine. Bring to a boil and cook over low heat 15 minutes. Mix in the clams and juice; cook 5 minutes longer.

Place a slice of toast in each plate, pour the clam soup over it and sprinkle with parsley.

SERVES : 4

Gambe di Rane, Salsa Prezzemolo

FROG'S LEGS WITH LEMON AND
PARSLEY SAUCE

24 small frog's legs
3 cups water
¼ cup vinegar
½ cup flour
1½ teaspoons salt
¼ teaspoon freshly ground black pepper
½ cup vegetable oil
3 tablespoons butter
1 clove garlic, minced
¼ cup lemon juice
3 tablespoons minced parsley

Have the frog's legs trimmed. Wash, then soak in the water and vinegar 2 hours. Rinse, drain and dry well. Dip the legs in a mixture of the flour, salt and pepper.

Heat the oil in a skillet; cook the legs in it 8 minutes, or until browned on all sides. Remove the legs to a hot serving dish and keep warm. Pour off the oil from the skillet. Melt the butter in the skillet. When lightly browned, mix in the garlic, then the lemon juice and parsley. Pour over the frog's legs and serve immediately.

SERVES : 4–6

Scampi alla Griglia

GRILLED SCAMPI OR SHRIMP

Scampi are native to Adriatic and parts of the Mediterranean. In some parts of the United States they are available frozen, but large shrimp may be used as a substitute.

    2 pounds raw scampi or shrimp
    ¾ cup olive oil
    ¾ teaspoon salt
    ½ teaspoon freshly ground black pepper
    2 cloves garlic, minced
    3 tablespoons minced parsley

Wash the seafood; shell and devein. Drain well.

Mix together the oil, salt, pepper, garlic and parsley. Marinate the scampi in the mixture 1 hour, basting and turning frequently. Remove shrimp and thread them on four or six wooden skewers or long toothpicks. Arrange on a baking sheet. Broil 10 minutes, turning the skewers and basting with the marinade several times. Serve immediately with lemon wedges.

SERVES : 4–6

Scampi alla Griglia Romeo

BUTTERFLY SHRIMP AND SAUCE

Sauce:

    2 tablespoons olive oil
    ½ cup chopped onions

1½ tablespoons dry mustard
⅓ cup wine vinegar
1 cup beef broth
1 cup Tomato Sauce (see recipe, p. 168)

Heat the oil in a saucepan; sauté the onions 5 minutes. Blend in the mustard, then mix in the vinegar and broth. Bring to a boil and cook over low heat 5 minutes. Stir in the tomato sauce; cook over low heat 10 minutes. Taste for seasoning. While the sauce is cooking, prepare the shrimp.

Shrimp:

2 pounds raw jumbo shrimp, shelled and deveined
½ cup olive oil
1½ teaspoons salt
½ teaspoon freshly ground black pepper
¾ cup dry bread crumbs

Wash and dry the shrimp. Dip in the olive oil, season with salt and pepper, then roll in the bread crumbs. Arrange on an oiled broiling pan. Broil until browned on both sides. Pour the sauce into small deep bowls and arrange shrimp around them.

SERVES : 4-6

Scampi alla Ciociara

SHRIMP IN CREAM

3 tablespoons olive oil
3 tablespoons butter
¼ cup minced onion
2 tablespoons grated carrot
1 bay leaf, finely chopped
1½ pounds raw shrimp, shelled and deveined
⅓ cup warm brandy

1 cup peeled chopped tomatoes
1 teaspoon salt
¼ teaspoon freshly ground black pepper
1 tablespoon lemon juice
¾ cup bottled clam juice
1 teaspoon flour
¾ cup heavy cream

Heat the oil and 2 tablespoons butter in a skillet; sauté the onion, carrot and bay leaf 10 minutes. Add the shrimp; sauté 3 minutes. Pour the warm brandy over the shrimp and set it aflame. When flames die, add the tomatoes, salt, pepper, lemon juice and clam juice. Cook over low heat 8 minutes.

Remove the shrimp to a warm serving dish. Cook the sauce over high heat 2 minutes. Knead the flour with the remaining butter and add to the sauce with the cream. Cook over low heat 3 minutes, stirring steadily. Pour over the shrimp.

SERVES : 4–6

Gamberoni Indiavolati

BRANDIED CRAYFISH

2 pounds raw crayfish or large shrimp
1 cup water
¼ cup brandy
2 carrots, sliced
1 onion
1 clove garlic
1½ teaspoons salt
¼ teaspoon thyme
1 bay leaf
Mayonnaise

Wash the crayfish or shrimp, shell and devein. In a saucepan, combine the water, brandy, carrots, onion, garlic, salt, thyme, bay leaf and seafood. Bring to a boil and cook over low heat 8 minutes. Let cool in the liquid. Drain thoroughly and serve coated with mayonnaise.

SERVES : 4–6

Aragosta al Forno

BAKED LOBSTER

2 1½-pound lobsters
1 teaspoon dry mustard
½ teaspoon freshly ground black pepper
1 tablespoon chopped parsley
½ teaspoon oregano
½ teaspoon salt
4 tablespoons olive oil
2 tablespoons melted butter
3 tablespoons bread crumbs
Lemon wedges

Split the lobsters lengthwise, remove black vein and sack. Place in a greased baking dish, shell side down. Mix together the mustard, pepper, parsley, oregano, salt, 2 tablespoons oil and the melted butter and spread on the lobster meat. Sprinkle with the bread crumbs and remaining olive oil and bake in a 375° oven 20 minutes. Serve with lemon wedges.

SERVES : 2–4

Aragosta alla Fiamma

LOBSTER PIQUANT

2 1½-pound live lobsters
½ cup olive oil
1 cup chopped onions
2 cloves garlic, minced

¼ cup brandy
1¼ teaspoons salt
½ teaspoon freshly ground black pepper
3 tablespoons tomato paste
½ teaspoon meat extract
¼ teaspoon oregano
¼ teaspoon saffron
½ cup dry white wine
1 teaspoon prepared mustard
2 tablespoons minced parsley

The lobsters may be cooked in the shell or not, as you prefer. Have the lobsters cut up, bodies in thirds and claws in half. Heat the oil until it boils in a deep skillet or casserole; add the lobster pieces and cook over high heat 5 minutes. Remove the lobster pieces and pour off half the oil. To the oil remaining, add the onions and garlic. Cook 5 minutes. Return the lobsters. Warm the brandy, set aflame and pour over the lobsters. When flames die, season with the salt and pepper. Mix together the tomato paste, meat extract, oregano, saffron and wine. Mix into the pan juices. Cover and cook over low heat 15 minutes. Arrange lobster pieces on a heated serving dish. Stir the mustard and parsley into the sauce. Pour over the lobsters.

SERVES : 2–4

Aragosta alla Diavola

LOBSTER DIAVOLA

2 1½-pound live lobsters, split
2 tablespoons butter
1 teaspoon salt
⅛ teaspoon cayenne pepper
Dash nutmeg
½ cup brandy
2 egg yolks
3 tablespoons heavy cream

Wash the lobsters, remove the meat and cut in large cubes. Dry. Melt the butter in a skillet; sauté the lobster meat 5 minutes. Season with the salt, cayenne pepper and nutmeg. Heat the brandy in a ladle, set it aflame and pour over the lobster. When flames die, cook the lobster over low heat 5 minutes longer.

Beat the egg yolks and cream; very gradually stir it into the skillet. Be sure to stir steadily, and cook only until sauce thickens, but do not let mixture boil. Serve with a plain *risotto*.

SERVES : 2–4

Aragosta Fra Diavolo Romeo

LOBSTER IN RED SAUCE

12 littleneck clams
2 1½-pound live lobsters
¼ cup olive oil
2 whole cloves garlic
¼ cup cognac
2 pounds tomatoes, peeled and chopped
1½ teaspoons salt
⅛ teaspoon crushed dried red pepper
½ teaspoon oregano
Chopped parsley

Scrub the clams and wash under cold running water. Wash the lobsters, chop off the claws and crack them. Split the bodies in half, remove the black vein and sack, then cut each half in half crosswise. (The fish man can do this for you, if you prefer.)

Heat the oil in a casserole or deep skillet. Place the garlic and lobsters in it, flesh side down. Cook until garlic browns, then discard it. Add the cognac; cover and cook 2 minutes. Add the tomatoes, salt, red pepper and oregano. Cook over medium heat 15 minutes. Add the clams, cover and cook 10 minutes longer. Sprinkle with the parsley and serve with sautéed Italian bread.

SERVES : 2–4

Pasta

SPAGHETTI AND NOODLES

Pasta, those delicious strands or shapes of dough, are beloved not only by Italians, but almost equally by Americans. In northern Italy, pasta was once regarded with condescension, but in the past few decades there has been an increased degree of popularity evinced for pasta dishes. Of course, in the northern part of the country, rice dishes are still highly regarded, and a *risotto* may still be preferred to any pasta.

But pasta is superb, the most delicious of all foods, many Italians think. It must be properly prepared, however. Use a very large pot; fill it with cold, fresh water, using at least four quarts of water to cook a pound of pasta. Add a tablespoon of salt to the water. Don't add the pasta until the water is actively boiling, then put it in gently, and do not break the strands if the pasta is of the long type. In a moment, it will soften, and the upper portion may be nudged into the boiling water. If you wish, add a teaspoon of olive oil to the water; this will prevent sticking.

Follow the cooking time given in the recipes for homemade pasta, or those of the manufacturer, if bought pasta is used. Never

61

overcook pasta—it will become pasty and doughy. It is best cooked *al dente*, which means literally "to the tooth," an untranslatable phrase which means that it should offer a slight degree of resistance to the tooth, but should not be tough.

Remember, too, that pasta can only be checked by tasting a strand or two every few minutes while it is cooking. When ready, remove from the heat immediately. The pasta will naturally continue to cook in the water even after being removed from the heat, so drain immediately, or add some cold water to the pot. (I do not recommend draining and rinsing with cold water; this will make the pasta cold.) Shake the pasta into a large colander at once, and see that all the water drains out. Don't delay, but serve the pasta and sauce immediately.

Incidentally, almost all pastas taste best with freshly-grated cheese. All Americans are accustomed to buying grated cheese in small glass containers, and these are adequate, but add less flavor. Buy a small piece of Parmesan or Romano cheese and grate it yourself just before using; the difference in flavor is worth the effort.

Pasta alla Uovo

EGG NOODLE DOUGH

4 cups sifted flour
1 teaspoon salt
4 eggs
1 tablespoon vegetable oil

Sift the flour and salt onto a board. Make a well in the center and into it put the eggs and oil. Work in the flour with the fingers until a firm dough is formed. Then knead the dough until very smooth and elastic. This will take about 10–15 minutes. Cover the dough with a bowl and let it rest for 20 minutes. This makes it easier to roll.

Divide the dough into three pieces. Lightly flour a board and roll out the dough as thin as possible, the thinner the better. Cut as described below. If all the noodles are not to be used at once, store in a tightly closed container.

Fettuccine:

Sprinkle the thinly rolled-out dough lightly with flour and cut into ½-inch wide strips. Spread on a clean cloth and let dry for about 1 hour. Cook in a deep pot of boiling salted water. Drain well and serve with a sauce or melted better.

Cannelloni:

Cut thinly rolled-out dough into 4-inch squares. Cook few squares at a time in deep boiling salted water 2 minutes. Remove with slotted spoon and drop into cold salted water. Drain and dry on cloth towel. Fill as desired, roll up, arrange in baking dish, cover with a selected sauce, and bake in a 400° oven 15 minutes.

Lasagne:

Sprinkle the thinly rolled-out dough with flour. Cut into strips 6 inches long and 2 inches wide. Cook in deep salted water 4 minutes. Drain well and use as directed in recipes.

Tagliatelle:

Prepare as for fettuccine, but cut into ¼-inch wide strips.

Lasagna Verde alla Bolognese

GREEN NOODLES WITH MEAT SAUCE

¼ pound butter
2 tablespoons olive oil
½ cup chopped onions

½ pound ground beef
1½ teaspoons salt
½ teaspoon freshly ground black pepper
½ cup dry white wine
3 tablespoons tomato sauce
½ cup water
1 pound green noodles, cooked and drained

Heat the butter and oil in a saucepan; sauté the onions 10 minutes. Mix in the meat until browned. Add the salt, pepper, wine and tomato sauce. Cook over low heat 1 hour, adding the water from time to time.

In a casserole or baking dish, arrange successive layers of the noodles and sauce, starting with the noodles and ending with the sauce. Bake in a 375° oven 15 minutes.

SERVES : 4–6

Spaghettini Zingarella

SPAGHETTI WITH WHITE CLAM SAUCE

36 small hard shell clams
¼ cup olive oil
4 whole cloves garlic
¼ teaspoon freshly ground black pepper
¼ teaspoon oregano
2 tablespoons minced parsley
¼ teaspoon basil
1 pound spaghettini, cooked and drained

Scrub the clams and rinse under cold running water until water runs clear.

Heat the oil in a saucepan; brown the garlic cloves in it, then discard. Add the clams, pepper, oregano, parsley and basil. Cover the pan and cook over low heat 10 minutes. Remove from the

heat and let stand 5 minutes before pouring over the hot, drained spaghettini.

SERVES : 4–6

Tagliatelle alla Salvatore

NOODLES WITH TOMATOES, CHEESE AND OLIVES

¼ pound butter
¼ cup olive oil
¾ cup chopped onions
1 20-ounce can tomatoes, sieved
1½ teaspoons salt
½ teaspoon freshly ground black pepper
1 teaspoon oregano
1 recipe egg noodle dough or 1 pound medium egg noodles, firmly cooked and drained
¼ cup grated Parmesan cheese
½ pound mozzarella cheese, cut in ¼-inch cubes
½ cup sliced black olives

Heat half the butter and the oil in a saucepan; sauté the onions 5 minutes. Add the tomatoes, salt and pepper; bring to a boil and cook over high heat 10 minutes. Mix in the oregano.

Melt the remaining butter in a casserole. Add the noodles, 2 tablespoons Parmesan cheese and the mozzarella. Toss well. Pour the sauce over the mixture, sprinkle with the remaining Parmesan cheese and arrange the olives on top. Bake in a 350° oven 10 minutes or until the mozzarella cheese begins to melt.

SERVES : 4–6

Tagliatelle alla Panna

EGG NOODLES WITH CREAM

1 cup heavy cream
2 tablespoons butter
1 recipe egg noodle dough or 1 pound medium egg noodles,
    cooked and drained
1 cup grated Parmesan cheese

Put half the cream and butter in a saucepan placed over low heat. Add the hot noodles and toss lightly with two forks. Add the cheese and the remaining cream and butter. Lift and toss the noodles until well coated. Serve very hot.

SERVES : 4–6

Pasta e Lenticchie

NOODLES WITH LENTILS

1 cup lentils
1½ cups peeled diced potatoes
½ pound tomatoes, chopped
½ cup chopped onions
2 tablespoons olive oil
2 teaspoons salt
¼ teaspoon freshly ground black pepper
¼ teaspoon dried sage
4 cups water
½ pound noodles (*ditalini, anellini,* if available)

Wash the lentils, cover with water, bring to a boil and let soak 1 hour. Drain. Add the potatoes, tomatoes, onions, oil, salt, pepper, sage and the 4 cups water. Bring to a boil and cook over low heat 1 hour; stirring occasionally. Mash ingredients lightly. Bring to an active boil and mix in the noodles. Cook over medium heat 12 minutes or until noodles are tender. Taste for seasoning.

Most of the liquid should be absorbed. Serve with grated cheese, if desired, but it's not necessary.

SERVES : 4–6

Pasta e Piselli

NOODLES WITH PEAS

2 tablespoons butter
4 slices bacon, diced
1 pound green peas, shelled or 1 package frozen, thawed peas
½ cup chopped onions
1 cup water
½ teaspoon salt
⅛ teaspoon sugar
⅛ teaspoon meat extract
1 cup grated Parmesan cheese
1 pound noodles, cooked and drained

In a skillet, combine the butter, bacon, peas, onions and water. Bring to a boil, cover, and cook over low heat 20 minutes, or until peas are very soft and water almost absorbed. Season with the salt, sugar and meat extract.

In a bowl, toss the cheese with the hot noodles, then with the green pea mixture.

SERVES : 4–6

Tagliatelle al Ragu

EGG NOODLES WITH MEAT SAUCE,
BOLOGNA FASHION

4 tablespoons butter
¾ cup chopped onions
¼ cup chopped celery

½ cup grated carrots
¼ pound prosciutto or cooked ham, cut julienne
¾ pound ground beef
2 tablespoons tomato paste
¾ cup dry red wine
1½ cups water
1 teaspoon salt
½ teaspoon freshly ground black pepper
1 recipe egg noodle dough or 1 pound medium egg noodles,
    cooked and drained
Grated Parmesan cheese

Melt the butter in a saucepan; sauté the onions, celery,
carrots and ham 10 minutes, stirring frequently. Add the meat;
cook 20 minutes, stirring frequently. Mix the tomato paste with
the wine and add to the saucepan with the water, salt and pepper.
Cover and cook over low heat 45 minutes. Mix a few times. Taste
for seasoning. Pour over the hot noodles and serve with grated
cheese.

SERVES : 4

Tagliatelle alla Bolognese con Prosciutto

EGG NOODLES WITH HAM

4 tablespoons butter
¼ pound prosciutto, cut julienne
½ noodle dough recipe, or ½ pound medium egg noodles,
    cooked and drained
1 cup grated Parmesan cheese

Melt the butter in a skillet; sauté the ham 3 minutes. Toss
the hot noodles with the cheese, then with the ham and butter
sauce.

SERVES : 2–6

Lasagne con Pesto

WIDE NOODLES WITH HERB SAUCE

8 fresh basil leaves or ¾ teaspoon dried basil
4 tablespoons minced parsley
2 cloves garlic, minced
1 cup grated Pecorino or Parmesan cheese
¼ cup olive oil
½ teaspoon freshly ground black pepper
1 recipe lasagne or 1 pound packaged lasagne, cooked and
    drained

Make an effort to get fresh basil if it's at all possible. If not, soak the dried basil in lukewarm water for 5 minutes to develop the flavor. Drain.

In a mortar with pestle, or on a board with a sharp knife, pound together the basil, parsley and garlic until very fine. Gradually add the cheese and oil alternately, pounding all the while. Mix in the pepper. Toss with the hot lasagne. Any other pasta may be served in the same manner.

SERVES : 4–6

Timballo Verde "Rispah"

TIMBALE OF GREEN NOODLES

2 dried mushrooms
4 tablespoons butter
¼ pound sweetbreads, parboiled and cubed
⅛ pound ham, cubed
¼ pound chicken livers, diced
1 cup Bolognese Sauce, strained
½ cup Tomato Sauce (see recipe, p. 168)
2 truffles, sliced

1 cup Besciamella (white) Sauce (see recipe, p. 173)
1 pound green noodles, cooked and drained
1 cup grated Parmesan cheese
4 tablespoons dry bread crumbs

Soak the mushrooms in water 10 minutes. Drain and slice.

Melt the butter in a skillet; stir in the sweetbreads, ham, livers and mushrooms. Sauté 5 minutes. Add the Bolognese and Tomato sauces; cook over low heat 10 minutes. Taste for seasoning. Mix in the truffles. Remove about ⅓ of this sauce and reserve.

Combine the balance of the sauce with the Besciamella, the noodles and half the Parmesan cheese. Mix thoroughly.

Butter 4–6 individual baking dishes and sprinkle with the bread crumbs. Divide the noodle mixture among them. Cover with the reserved sauce and sprinkle with remaining cheese. Bake in a preheated 375° oven 10 minutes.

SERVES : 4–6

Ravioli or Tortellini

Ravioli are square, and tortellini are small snail-shaped dough pockets. The fillings and dough are interchangeable.

Dough:

4 cups sifted flour
1 teaspoon salt
3 eggs
4 tablespoons cold water

Sift the flour and salt into a bowl. Make a well in the center and into it put the eggs and water. With the fingers, blend all together until a ball of dough is formed. If too dry, add a little more water. If too wet, add a little more flour.

Turn out onto a floured surface and knead until very smooth and elastic. Flour the surface and hands occasionally. Cover with a bowl and let rest 20 minutes.

Ravioli:

Divide dough in half and roll out and stretch ⅛-inch thick and cut into long strips 2-inches wide. Place a heaping teaspoon of filling at 2-inch intervals. Cover with another strip of dough. Using the index finger, press down around the filling. Use a pastry wheel or sharp knife and cut into 2-inch squares. Seal the edges carefully. Let stand 2 hours before cooking. If you prefer, cut dough into 2-inch squares, place filling in the center and cover with another square.

Tortellini:

Divide dough in half, roll out and stretch ⅛-inch thick. Cut into 1½-inch circles. Place a half teaspoon of filling in the center. Fold each circle in half, to form a half circle, but the top part should come just short of the bottom. Press edges firmly together, then bring the ends together, so that it forms a ring. Let dry 3 hours before cooking.

To cook ravioli or tortellini, drop them into deep boiling, salted water. Cook 7 minutes, or until they rise to the top. Remove with a slotted spoon. Serve with melted butter and grated cheese or with a sauce. Tortellini may also be served in soup.

Cannelloni, Ravioli and Tortellini Fillings

Meat:

2 tablespoons butter
1½ cups ground cooked beef or veal
¼ cup grated Parmesan cheese

¼ cup dry bread crumbs
⅛ teaspoon nutmeg

Melt the butter in a skillet; sauté the meat 5 minutes. Cool and mix in the cheese, bread crumbs and nutmeg. Taste for seasoning.

Spinach-Meat:

¾ cup cooked chopped spinach, drained thoroughly
¾ cup ground cooked meat
¼ cup grated Parmesan cheese
⅛ teaspoon nutmeg
3 tablespoons dry bread crumbs

Mix all the ingredients together and taste for seasoning.

Spinach-Cheese:

1 cup cooked chopped spinach, drained thoroughly
½ cup ricotta or cottage cheese, drained
¼ cup grated Parmesan cheese
3 tablespoons dry bread crumbs

Mix all the ingredients together and taste for seasoning.

Bologna:

½ cup sausage meat
1 tablespoon butter
1 cup ground cooked pork
¾ cup grated Parmesan cheese
1 egg yolk
3 tablespoons dry bread crumbs
⅛ teaspoon nutmeg

Brown the sausage meat. Pour off the fat. Add the butter and pork; cook 5 minutes. Cool and mix in the cheese, egg yolk, bread crumbs and nutmeg. Taste for seasoning.

Spaghetti Piatto Unico

SPAGHETTI WITH VEAL DUMPLINGS

½ pound ground veal
⅛ pound prosciutto, or cooked ham, finely chopped
2 tablespoons grated Parmesan cheese
1½ teaspoons salt
1 egg, beaten
½ cup dry bread crumbs
3 tablespoons butter
2 tablespoons dry vermouth
1 pound tomatoes, chopped
¼ teaspoon freshly ground black pepper
1 pound spaghetti, cooked and drained

Mix together the veal, ham, cheese, ½ teaspoon salt and the egg. Shape teaspoons of the mixture into little balls. Roll in the bread crumbs.

Melt the butter in a saucepan; brown the balls in it. Add the wine; cook until absorbed, add the tomatoes, pepper and remaining salt; cook over low heat 30 minutes. Taste for seasoning. Pour over the hot spaghetti and serve with grated cheese. This dish is served as a main course.

SERVES : 4

Lasagne al Forno

BAKED LASAGNE

4 tablespoons butter
2 tablespoons flour
1½ teaspoons salt
¾ cup milk
½ pound chicken livers, diced
½ pound Italian sausages, skinned and chopped
2 tablespoons olive oil
1 recipe lasagne dough or 1 pound lasagne, cooked and drained
3 cups Tomato Sauce (see recipe, page 168)
½ pound prosciutto, or cooked ham, chopped
1½ cups grated Parmesan cheese

Melt 2 tablespoons of the butter in a saucepan; blend in the flour and half the salt. Add the milk, stirring steadily to the boiling point, then cook over low heat 5 minutes.

Melt 1 tablespoon of the butter in a skillet; sauté the livers 2 minutes. Add the sausage meat and remaining salt and cook 10 minutes. Drain.

Oil a shallow baking dish and make a layer of lasagne. Arrange as many succesive layers as possible of the Tomato Sauce, sausage mixture, white sauce, ham and grated cheese. End with lasagne and grated cheese. Dot with the remaining butter. Bake in a 400° oven 15 minutes or until browned. Cut into squares and serve from the dish.

SERVES : 4–6

Pasta Gratinata

BAKED MACARONI AND CHEESE

6 tablespoons butter
4 tablespoons flour
2 cups milk
1 teaspoon salt
¼ teaspoon white pepper
¾ pound macaroni, cooked and drained
1 cup grated Parmesan cheese

Melt 4 tablespoons of the butter in a saucepan; blend in the flour. Add the milk, stirring steadily to the boiling point. Mix in the salt and pepper. Cook over low heat 10 minutes.

In a greased casserole, make as many layers as possible of the macaroni, cheese and sauce. Dot with the remaining butter. Bake in a 400° oven 20 minutes.

SERVES : 3–4

Pasta ai Tre Formaggi

MACARONI WITH THREE CHEESES

1 pound macaroni
3 tablespoons butter
1 cup grated Parmesan cheese
½ cup grated Gruyère or Swiss cheese
½ cup grated fontina or mozzarella cheese
1 cup heavy cream

Use any shape macaroni you like. Cook in deep, boiling, salted water until tender but still firm. Drain, rinse under cold water and drain again.

In a casserole, toss the macaroni with the butter, then the three cheeses. Add the cream. Bake in a 400° oven 20 minutes or until browned.

SERVES : 4–6

Maccheroni con la Ricotta

MACARONI WITH RICOTTA

½ pound ricotta or cottage cheese
¾ teaspoon salt
¼ teaspoon freshly ground black pepper
⅛ teaspoon nutmeg
3 tablespoons hot water
1 pound macaroni, cooked and drained
Grated Parmesan cheese

In a bowl, mix together the ricotta, salt, pepper and nutmeg. Beat in the hot water. Toss with the hot macaroni and serve with grated Parmesan cheese.

SERVES : 4–6

Spaghetti alla Ghiotta

SPAGHETTI WITH PEAS AND TRUFFLES

3 tablespoons butter
2 cups drained canned green peas
2 truffles, thinly sliced
½ teaspoon freshly ground black pepper
1 pound spaghetti, cooked and drained
½ cup grated Parmesan cheese

Melt the butter in a saucepan; add the peas, truffles and pepper. Cook over low heat 5 minutes. Add to the hot spaghetti with the cheese. Toss together lightly. Serve with Tomato Sauce on the side, if desired.

SERVES : 4–6

Spaghetti alla Marinara

SPAGHETTI WITH TOMATO SAUCE

¼ cup olive oil
2 cloves garlic, split
1½ pounds tomatoes, peeled and diced
1½ teaspoons salt
½ teaspoon freshly ground black pepper
3 tablespoons minced parsley
1 pound spaghetti, cooked and drained
Grated Parmesan cheese (optional)

Heat the oil in a saucepan; brown the garlic in it, then discard. Add the tomatoes, salt and pepper; cook over low heat 20 minutes, or until liquid is almost evaporated. Taste for seasoning. Mix in the parsley. Pour over the hot spaghetti and serve with grated cheese, if desired.

SERVES : 4–6

Spaghetti all' Amatriciana

SPAGHETTI WITH BACON SAUCE

¼ pound bacon, diced
½ cup chopped onion
¼ cup dry white wine
1 pound tomatoes, peeled and chopped
½ teaspoon freshly ground black pepper
1 pound spaghetti, cooked and drained
1 cup grated Pecorino or Parmesan cheese

In a saucepan, cook the bacon and onion until browned. Add the wine; cook until almost evaporated. Mix in the tomatoes and pepper; cook over low heat 20 minutes. Taste for seasoning. Pour over the hot spaghetti and sprinkle with the cheese.

SERVES : 4–6

Spaghetti alla Carbonara

SPAGHETTI WITH HAM—EGG SAUCE

3 slices bacon, cut julienne
4 tablespoons butter
½ cup julienne-cut prosciutto
2 egg yolks
1 cup grated Parmesan cheese
1 pound spaghetti, cooked and drained

Brown the bacon in the butter; mix in the ham until lightly browned.

Beat the egg yolks, then stir in ¼ cup of the cheese. Toss the hot spaghetti with bacon mixture, then immediately with the egg yolk mixture. Serve quickly sprinkled with the remaining cheese.

SERVES : 4–6

Spaghetti Aglio e Olio

SPAGHETTI WITH OIL, GARLIC AND PARSLEY

½ cup olive oil
4 whole cloves garlic
1 pound spaghettini (thin spaghetti) cooked and drained
¼ cup minced parsley

Heat the oil in a skillet; brown the garlic in it and discard. Pour the oil over the hot drained spaghettini; sprinkle with the parsley and toss lightly.

SERVES : 4

Gnocchi di Patate

POTATO DUMPLINGS

2 pounds potatoes
2 egg yolks
1½ teaspoons salt
1⅛ cups flour (about)
1 tablespoon melted butter

Buy firm dry potatoes. Scrub the potatoes and cook in boiling water until tender. Drain and peel. Return potatoes to the saucepan and shake over low heat until dry. Mash the potatoes very smooth. Mix in the egg yolks and salt. Add just enough of the flour to make a dough. This depends on the moisture in the potatoes. Mix in the butter.

On a lightly-floured surface, roll the dough into finger-thick rolls. Cut into 1-inch lengths. Cook in boiling, salted water until they rise to the surface, about 10 minutes. Remove with a slotted spoon. Serve with melted butter and grated cheese, or with a sauce.

SERVES : 4–6

Gnocchi Romani

SEMOLINA DUMPLINGS

4 cups milk
⅛ teaspoon nutmeg
1 teaspoon salt
6 tablespoons butter
1¼ cups semolina or Cream of Wheat
3 eggs
1 cup grated Romano or Parmesan cheese

Bring the milk, salt, nutmeg and 1 tablespoon butter to a
boil. Gradually add the semolina or Cream of Wheat, stirring stirring steadily with a wooden spoon until thickened, then cook 10
minutes longer. Remove from heat. Beat in the eggs and ¼ cup of
the cheese. Pour into a buttered pan to a depth of ½-inch or spread
on a wet board ½-inch thick. Chill. Cut into 1-inch circles or
squares.

Melt the remaining butter.

In a shallow buttered baking dish arrange layers of the gnocchi, sprinkling each layer with melted butter and cheese. Bake in
a 400° oven 10 minutes or until browned.

SERVES : 4–6

Gnocchi alla Ricotta

RICOTTA DUMPLINGS

1 pound ricotta or cottage cheese
2 cups sifted flour
3 eggs
1 tablespoon melted butter
1 cup grated Parmesan cheese
½ cup melted browned butter

Drain the cheese, pressing out all the liquid, then force it
through a sieve. Work in the flour, eggs, and butter, then half the

cheese. Knead until a dough is formed. (If too soft, add a little more flour.) Cover with a bowl and let stand 1 hour. Form into finger-thick rolls and cut in 1-inch lengths. Cook in boiling salted water 10 minutes. Remove with a slotted spoon and sprinkle with the browned butter and remaining cheese.

SERVES : 4-6

Gnocchi Verdi

SPINACH—CHEESE DUMPLINGS

½ pound ricotta or cottage cheese
2 pounds spinach or 2 packages frozen, thawed
3 egg yolks
2 cups freshly grated Parmesan cheese
⅛ teaspoon nutmeg
Flour
½ cup melted browned butter

Press all the liquid from the ricotta or cottage cheese—it must be very dry.

Bring the spinach to a boil in salted water and drain thoroughly at once. Purée in an electric blender or chop very fine. Drain again if necessary.

Beat the egg yolks, then mix in the drained cheese, spinach, 1 cup Parmesan cheese and the nutmeg.

Knead on a floured surface until smooth. Let stand 30 minutes. Shape into finger-thick rolls, then cut into 1-inch lengths. Roll in flour.

Use a large deep skillet and almost fill it with water. Bring to a boil and reduce heat to low. Carefully add the dumplings one at a time. Cook over low heat until they rise to the surface. Drain well. Pour the melted butter over them and sprinkle with the remaining Parmesan cheese.

SERVES : 6-8

Gnocchi Mamma Siepi

SPINACH ROLL

Filling:

1 pound spinach or 1 package frozen spinach
½ pound ricotta cheese, drained
½ cup grated Parmesan cheese
¼ teaspoon nutmeg
¼ teaspoon freshly ground black pepper

Cook the spinach, then drain thoroughly and chop fine.
Mix in the ricotta, Parmesan, nutmeg and pepper until smooth.

Dough:

2 pounds potatoes
2 egg yolks
1½ teaspoons salt
2 cups flour (about)
1 tablespoon melted butter

Buy firm, dry potatoes. Scrub the potatoes and cook in
boiling water until tender. Drain and peel. Return potatoes to the
saucepan and shake over low heat until dry. Mash the potatoes
very smooth. Mix in the egg yolks and salt. Add just enough of
the flour to make a dough. This depends on the moisture in the
potatoes. Mix in the butter. Knead until smooth. Roll out on a
lightly-floured surface into a thin 14-inch square. Spread the filling about ½-inch thick. Roll up like a jelly roll. Place in a napkin
or piece of cheesecloth, completely covering the roll. Carefully
lower into boiling water and cook 30 minutes. Remove carefully
from water, unwrap and drain roll. Cut into ¾-inch slices, transfer
to a heated platter and serve with Tomato Sauce, Bolognese Sauce
(see recipes) or melted butter and grated Parmesan cheese.

SERVES : 4–6

Polenta Pasticciata alla Milanese

CORN MEAL AND CHEESE PIE

1 quart water
1½ teaspoons salt
1 cup yellow corn meal
3 tablespoons bread crumbs
2 cups grated fontina or mozzarella cheese
6 tablespoons butter

Bring the water and salt to a boil; stir in the corn meal until it begins to thicken. Cook over low heat 20 minutes, stirring frequently.

Grease a shallow baking dish and sprinkle with the bread crumbs. Spread ¼ of the corn meal in it; cover with ¼ of the cheese and dot with ¼ of the butter. Repeat the layers until all the ingredients are used up. Bake in a 375° oven 15 minutes or until browned.

SERVES : 4–6

Pizza alla Casalinga

HOME-STYLE PIZZA

½ envelope yeast
¼ cup lukewarm water
1½ cups flour
2 teaspoons salt
4 tablespoons butter
1 egg, beaten
4 cups peeled diced tomatoes or canned drained tomatoes
½ teaspoon black pepper
½ cup olive oil
2 cans anchovy fillets
1 teaspoon oregano
½ pound mozzarella cheese, thinly sliced

Soften the yeast in the water. Sift the flour and 1 teaspoon salt into a bowl. Work in the butter with the fingers. Add the egg to the yeast, then stir into the flour mixture until a ball of dough is formed. If too stiff, add a little more water. Knead on a lightly-floured surface until smooth and elastic. Form into a ball, place in an oiled bowl, cover with a towel and let rise in a warm place for 2 hours.

Divide the dough into two pieces and roll out each piece to fit an 8-inch (greased) pie plate. Spread each with tomatoes, season with the remaining salt and the pepper, sprinkle with some olive oil; arrange anchovies over tomatoes and sprinkle with the oregano. Bake in a 400° oven 20 minutes. Arrange the cheese on top and bake 5 minutes longer or until dough is browned and cheese melted. Serve hot, cut into wedges.

SERVES : 4–8

Variations:

In place of the anchovies and mozzarella you may use one of the following:

Flaked tunafish
Sliced sausages
Tiny meat balls
Thinly sliced ham

Sprinkle top with grated Parmesan cheese, if desired.

Pizza di Patate

POTATO PIZZA

Potato Gnocchi recipe
1 cup vegetable oil
¼ pound mozzarella cheese, thinly sliced

1 cup Tomato Sauce (see recipe, page 168)
½ cup grated Parmesan cheese

Roll out the potato dough 1-inch thick. Cut into 2-inch rounds. Using the hands, pat the dough thin, so as to double the size of the rounds.

In a skillet, bring the oil to a boil. Fry a few rounds at a time until browned on the underside. Turn over and immediately place a slice of cheese on each. Fry until underside is browned and cheese melted. Remove with a skimmer onto absorbent paper. Sprinkle with a little Tomato Sauce and Parmesan cheese. Place on a plate and keep hot over boiling water while preparing the balance.

MAKES : ABOUT 12

Risotti

RICE DISHES

Rice preparations are extremely popular in the north, customarily being made into a *risotto*, which may roughly be translated as a "rice dish." Unlike the American use of rice, in which the plain, boiled variety is served with butter to accompany a main course, the Italians almost never do so. *Risotto* is cooked slowly with herbs and spices, meat or fish, or possibly with a sauce. The flavor is absorbed into each grain of rice gradually, and the final dish is truly a gastronomic treat. Because most restaurants in America are run by Italians who originated in southern Italy where pasta is the great favorite, very few Americans know about the delights of a *risotto*. *Risottos* vary from region to region, one district preparing the rice with a meat base, another with fish, generally dependent upon what is available and what is best in a particular locality.

The secret of a good risotto lies in the way the liquid is used. Small amounts of hot liquid should be added at a time, then cooked until absorbed. Continue until all is used up.

Risotto alla Milanese

RICE, MILAN STYLE

3 tablespoons butter
½ cup finely chopped onions
2 tablespoons beef marrow (optional)
2 cups raw long grain rice
¼ cup dry white wine
¼ teaspoon saffron
1 teaspoon salt
4½ cups boiling chicken broth
2 tablespoons minced parsley
½ cup grated Parmesan cheese

Melt 2 tablespoons butter in a saucepan; add the onions, and marrow, if used. Cook over low heat until onions are soft and yellow. Stir in the rice until yellow. Add the wine, saffron, and salt; cook until absorbed. Add 1 cup broth; cover and cook until absorbed. Continue adding 1 cup broth at a time, until rice is tender but firm. Stir in the remaining butter, then the parsley and cheese. Remove from heat and let stand covered, 5 minutes before serving.

SERVES : 4–6

Risotto di Scampi

SHRIMP RISOTTO

6 tablespoons butter
3 tablespoons olive oil
1 clove garlic, minced
1½ cups raw long grain rice
¾ cup dry white wine
3½ cups boiling chicken broth
1 pound cooked, cleaned shrimp
1½ teaspoons salt
¼ teaspoon white pepper
¼ teaspoon marjoram
3 tablespoons grated Parmesan cheese

Heat 4 tablespoons butter and the oil in a heavy skillet or casserole. Stir in the garlic and rice until golden. Add the wine; cook over medium heat until absorbed. Add half the broth; cover and cook over low heat 15 minutes. Add the shrimp, salt, pepper, marjoram and remaining broth. Stir lightly with a fork. Recover and cook 10 minutes over low heat or until rice is tender and dry. Stir in the cheese and remaining butter.

SERVES : 4–6

Risotto con Fegatini

RICE WITH CHICKEN LIVERS AND
MUSHROOM SAUCE

6 tablespoons butter
¾ cup finely chopped onions
2 cups raw long grain rice
⅛ cup Marsala or sweet sherry
5 cups hot chicken broth
1½ teaspoons salt
½ cup thinly sliced onion
½ cup julienne-cut prosciutto ham
¼ pound chicken livers, diced
½ pound mushrooms, sliced
1 cup beef broth
¼ teaspoon freshly ground black pepper
1 bay leaf
¼ teaspoon thyme

Melt half the butter in a saucepan; sauté the chopped onions until yellow and transparent. Stir in the rice until lightly browned. Add ¼ cup wine; cook until absorbed. Add 2 cups of the chicken broth and half the salt; cover and cook over low heat 25 minutes, adding the remaining chicken broth as it becomes absorbed by the rice. Meanwhile prepare the sauce.

Melt the remaining butter in a small saucepan; sauté the sliced onion and ham 5 minutes. Add the livers and mushrooms; sauté 5 minutes, stirring frequently. Mix in the beef broth, remaining salt, the pepper, bay leaf, thyme and remaining wine. Cook over low heat 10 minutes. Taste for seasoning. Discard the bay leaf, then mix half the sauce with the rice. Heap in a bowl and pour remaining sauce over the top.

SERVES : 4–6

Risi e Bisi

RICE AND PEAS, VENETIAN STYLE

4 tablespoons olive oil
4 tablespoons butter
¾ cup chopped onions
1½ cups raw long grain rice
3 tablespoons dry sherry
3 cups shelled fresh peas or 2 packages frozen, thawed peas
3 cups hot chicken broth
1½ teaspoons salt
¼ teaspoon white pepper
¼ cup grated Parmesan cheese

Heat the oil and 2 tablespoons butter in a heavy saucepan; sauté the onions 5 minutes. Mix in the rice until translucent. Add the sherry; cook over low heat 1 minute. Add the peas, 2 cups broth, salt and pepper. Cover, bring to a boil and cook over low heat 10 minutes. Add the remaining broth, recover and cook 10 minutes longer or until rice is tender and dry. Taste for seasoning; mix in the cheese and remaining butter.

SERVES : 6–8

Risoverdi

GREEN RICE

2 tablespoons olive oil
4 tablespoons butter
1 cup minced scallions (green onions)
1 cup minced parsley
1½ cups finely chopped raw spinach
2 cups raw long grain rice
3½ cups hot chicken broth
1½ teaspoons salt
¼ teaspoon white pepper
Grated Parmesan cheese

Heat the oil and 2 tablespoons butter in a heavy saucepan; mix in the scallions, parsley and spinach. Cover and cook over low heat 5 minutes. Mix in the rice until translucent. Add 2 cups broth, the salt and pepper; cover and cook over low heat 20 minutes, adding the remaining broth after 10 minutes. Lightly mix in the remaining butter with a fork. Serve with the cheese.

SERVES : 4–6

Risotto al Salto

RICE FRITTERS

6 tablespoons butter
½ cup finely chopped onions
2 cups raw long grain rice
¼ cup dry white wine
1 teaspoon salt
4½ cups boiling chicken broth
2 tablespoons minced parsley
½ cup grated Parmesan cheese
3 tablespoons olive oil

Melt 3 tablespoons butter in a saucepan; add the onions. Cook over low heat until onions are soft and golden-colored. Stir in the rice, continuing until rice is yellow. Add the wine and salt; cook until absorbed. Add 1 cup broth; cover and cook until absorbed. Continue adding 1 cup broth at a time; until rice is tender but firm. Remove from the heat. Stir in the remaining butter, parsley, and the cheese. Spread in a shallow pan, then chill.

Heat the olive oil in a skillet. Scoop out heaping tablespoons of the rice and place in the skillet. Cook over low heat until underside is browned. Flatten the rice balls very gently, being careful not to break them up, and turn over to brown other side. Serve very hot.

SERVES : 4–6

Lenticchie con Risotto

LENTILS AND RICE

1 cup lentils
4 tablespoons butter
½ cup chopped onions
3 cups beef broth
½ teaspoon freshly ground black pepper
2 cups cooked drained rice
1 cup grated Parmesan cheese

Wash the lentils, cover with water and bring to a boil. Let soak 30 minutes. Drain.

Melt half the butter in a saucepan; sauté the onions 10 minutes. Mix in the lentils, broth and pepper. Bring to a boil and cook over medium heat 1 hour. Drain, if any liquid remains. With a fork, stir in the rice, cheese and remaining butter. Taste for seasoning.

SERVES : 4–6

Riso e Verze alla Lombarda

RICE AND CABBAGE, LOMBARDY STYLE

3 slices bacon, diced
½ cup chopped onions
1 clove garlic, minced
2 pounds cabbage, shredded
3 cups beef broth
1 cup raw long grain rice
1½ teaspoons salt
2 tablespoons minced parsley
¼ cup grated Parmesan cheese

In a large saucepan, brown the bacon, onions and garlic. Add the shredded cabbage and cook 15 minutes, stirring frequently. Add the broth; cover and cook over low heat 1 hour. Mix in the rice and salt; recover and cook 20 minutes or until rice is tender but firm. With a fork, stir in the parsley and cheese. Taste for seasoning.

SERVES : 4–6

Riso a Dischetti

RICE DISKS

2 tablespoons butter
½ cup chopped onions
1 cup raw rice
1½ cups beef broth
1 teaspoon salt
2 eggs
4 tablespoons grated Parmesan cheese
⅛ pound Bel Paese cheese
¾ cup dry bread crumbs
2 cups vegetable oil

Melt the butter in a skillet; sauté the onions 5 minutes. Mix in the rice until lightly browned. Add ¾ cup of the broth and the salt. Cover and cook until broth is absorbed. Add remaining broth, recover and cook until rice is tender but firm and dry (about 18 minutes altogether). Let cool. Mix in 1 egg yolk (reserve white) and the grated cheese. Rinse a board with cold water and spread the rice on it to a thickness of about ¼-inch. When completely cold, cut into rounds about 2 inches in diameter. Slice the cheese very thin, then into rounds a little smaller than the rice. Make sandwiches of 2 rounds of rice with a round of cheese between. Press the edges together firmly. Beat the remaining egg with the reserved egg white. Dip the sandwiches in it, then in the bread crumbs, coating them thoroughly. Heat the oil in a skillet until it sizzles; fry the rounds in it until browned on both sides. Drain on absorbent paper and place in a hot oven for a few minutes. Serve hot.

SERVES : 4–6

Riso alla Genovese

RICE, GENOA STYLE

3 tablespoons olive oil
1 cup chopped onions
1 cup chopped celery
1 cup grated carrots
½ pound ground veal
2½ teaspoons salt
½ teaspoon freshly ground black pepper
¼ teaspoon rosemary
2 tablespoons minced parsley
¾ cup dry white wine
3 cups water
1½ cups raw long grain rice
2 tablespoons butter

Heat the oil in a saucepan; sauté the onions, celery and carrots 10 minutes. Mix in the veal, 1 teaspoon salt, pepper, rosemary and parsley; sauté 5 minutes, stirring frequently. Add the wine; cover and cook over low heat 50 minutes.

Meanwhile, cook the rice. Combine the water, rice and remaining salt in a saucepan; bring to a boil, cover and cook over low heat 15 minutes. Drain, if any water remains. Put in a clean saucepan and shake over low heat to dry. Mix in the butter and half the sauce; cook over low heat 5 minutes, stirring almost constantly. Transfer to a hot serving dish and cover with the remaining sauce. Serve with grated Parmesan cheese.

SERVES : 4–6

Risotto alla Montanara

RICE WITH BEANS,
MOUNTAINEER'S STYLE

1 slice bacon, diced
¾ cup finely chopped onions
1 stalk celery, chopped
1 cup peeled chopped tomatoes
2 cups cooked or canned kidney beans
1½ teaspoons salt
¼ teaspoon freshly ground black pepper
¼ teaspoon sage
¼ teaspoon rosemary
3 cups cooked drained rice
½ cup grated Parmesan cheese

In a saucepan, cook the bacon and onions until lightly browned. Add the celery, tomatoes, beans, salt, pepper, sage and rosemary. Cover and cook over low heat 45 minutes. Stir in the rice and cheese. Cook 2 minutes. Taste for seasoning.

SERVES : 4–6

Uova e Formaggio

EGGS AND CHEESE

I n my native country, eggs are almost never eaten for breakfast. And, unlike America where eggs are not very popular at lunch or dinner, they are very usual in Italy. It is a custom that I would like to see introduced in the United States, for there are few dishes so satisfying for lunch as a properly prepared egg dish.

Italians like *frittatas,* which are like omelets, but are usually served flat with a sauce. They should never be overcooked, and for that matter, should always be cooked over low heat, for eggs toughen quickly when prepared with high heat. For a novel first course, serve a *frittata* to your guests.

Frittata

VEGETABLE OMELET

3 tablespoons olive oil
½ cup chopped onions
½ cup sliced mushrooms
½ cup sliced zucchini

½ package frozen artichoke hearts, thawed
2 teaspoons salt
½ teaspoon freshly ground black pepper
6 eggs
¼ cup canned tomato sauce

Heat the oil in a skillet (with ovenproof handle); sauté the onions 5 minutes. Add the mushrooms, zucchini and artichokes; sauté 10 minutes. Season with half the salt and pepper.

Beat the eggs with the remaining salt and pepper; pour over the vegetables. Spoon the tomato sauce over the top. Bake in a preheated 350° oven 15 minutes or until set. Serve at once, cut in wedges. The *Frittata* may also be baked in individual dishes, in which case serve in the dish.

SERVES : 4-6

Frittata alla Ricotta

HAM—CHEESE OMELET

4 eggs
½ teaspoon salt
¼ teaspoon freshly ground black pepper
½ cup julienne-cut ham
½ cup ricotta or cottage cheese, drained
1 tablespoon butter
1 tablespoon olive oil

Beat together lightly the eggs, salt and pepper. Mix in the ham and cheese.

Heat the butter and oil in a 9-inch skillet. Pour in the egg mixture. Cook over medium heat, stirring with a fork for a few seconds, then lift the edges to allow the uncooked mixture to run under. Fold over and roll out the omelet onto a heated dish. Don't overcook the omelet.

SERVES : 2-3

Frittata al Formaggio

CHEESE OMELET

3 eggs
1 tablespoon water
⅛ teaspoon oregano
¼ teaspoon salt
⅛ teaspoon white pepper
½ cup diced Bel Paese cheese
1 tablespoon minced parsley
2 tablespoons butter
2 tablespoons olive oil

Beat the eggs, water, oregano, salt and pepper until just blended. Stir in the cheese and parsley.

Heat the butter and oil in a 9-inch skillet until it bubbles. Pour in the egg mixture; cook over medium heat until bottom browns lightly. Lift the edges to allow the unset part to run under, then turn over to brown other side. (Put a plate over the pan, and turn omelet onto it, then slide it back into the pan.) Turn out (flat) onto a heated serving dish.

SERVES : 2

Frittata Spumosa

FROTHY CHEESE OMELET

4 egg yolks
1½ tablespoons heavy cream
½ teaspoon salt
4 egg whites, beaten stiff
⅓ cup grated mozzarella or Swiss cheese
2 tablespoons butter

Beat the egg yolks, cream and salt lightly. Fold in the beaten egg whites and cheese.

Melt the butter in a 9-inch skillet; pour the egg mixture into it. Cook over low heat, shaking the pan constantly. Lift edges with a fork to allow uncooked eggs to run under. When fairly set, fold over and roll out onto a heated plate.

SERVES : 2–3

Frittata con Peperoni

GREEN PEPPER OMELET

2 tablespoons olive oil
½ cup chopped onions
1 cup chopped green peppers
¼ cup water
6 eggs
1¼ teaspoons salt
¼ teaspoon white pepper
3 tablespoons olive oil

Heat the oil in a saucepan; sauté the onions and green peppers for 5 minutes. Add the water and cook over very low heat until absorbed. Cool for 5 minutes.

Beat the eggs, salt and pepper; stir in the vegetables. Heat the oil in a skillet; lightly scramble the eggs in it.

SERVES : 3–4

Frittata col Tonno

OMELET WITH TUNA

4 eggs
⅛ teaspoon salt
¼ teaspoon pepper

1 teaspoon chopped parsley
½ teaspoon oregano
1 7¾-ounce can tuna fish, drained and flaked
1 clove garlic, minced
2 anchovy fillets, minced
2 tablespoons olive oil

In a bowl beat the eggs; mix in the salt, pepper, parsley, oregano, tuna fish, garlic and anchovies. Heat the oil in an 11-inch skillet; pour the egg mixture into it, cook over low heat 5 minutes on each side.

SERVES : 4–6

Frittatine Imbottite

STUFFED PANCAKES

Pancakes:

1 cup sifted flour
½ teaspoon salt
1 egg
½ cup milk
½ cup water
2 tablespoons vegetable oil
2 tablespoons butter

Sift the flour and salt into a bowl; beat in the egg, milk and water until smooth, then stir in the oil. Chill 2 hours. Beat again—the mixture should be like cream—if too thick, add a little more milk.

Melt a little butter in a 7-inch skillet; when it bubbles, pour in just enough batter to thinly coat the bottom, about 1 tablespoon. Cook just until set and lightly browned, then turn over. Stack while preparing the balance.

Filling:

¼ cup grated Swiss cheese
1 cup grated Parmesan cheese
1 egg, beaten
¼ cup milk
¼ teaspoon white pepper
¼ teaspoon nutmeg
3 tablespoons butter
½ cup light cream

Mix together the Swiss cheese, ½ cup Parmesan cheese, the egg, milk, pepper and nutmeg. Place a heaping tablespoon on each pancake and roll up. Arrange in a single layer, in a buttered shallow baking dish. Dot with the butter, sprinkle with the remaining cheese and add the cream. Bake in a preheated 350° oven 15 minutes or until browned.

M A K E S :   A B O U T   12

Uova in Tazzine con Spinaci

EGGS AND SPINACH IN CUPS

1 pound spinach, or 1 package frozen spinach
1 teaspoon salt
¼ teaspoon white pepper
⅛ teaspoon nutmeg
4 tablespoons heavy cream
4 teaspoons butter
4 slices prosciutto or cooked ham
4 eggs

Cook the spinach, drain very well and purée in an electric blender or force through a sieve. Mix in the salt, pepper, nutmeg and half the cream. Use four custard cups or individual baking dishes and in each melt 1 teaspoon butter. Spread a little spinach in each, place a slice of ham over it and cover with the remaining spinach. Make a slight impression in the center. Break an egg into each, but discard half the white. Season with salt and pepper, then add ½ tablespoon of the remaining cream to each.

Bake in a 400° oven 5 minutes or until eggs are cooked the way you like them.

SERVES : 4

Uova alla Cacciatora

EGGS, HUNTER'S STYLE

¼ pound chicken livers
4 tablespoons olive oil
¼ cup chopped onions
1¼ teaspoons salt
¼ teaspoon freshly ground black pepper
¼ teaspoon basil
¼ cup canned tomato sauce
¼ cup dry white wine
4 eggs
4 slices buttered toast
1 tablespoon parsley

Wash the livers, removing any discolored areas. Cut each half in 2 pieces.

Heat the oil in a skillet; sauté the onions 5 minutes. Add the livers; sauté 5 minutes, mixing a few times. Add the salt, pepper, basil, tomato sauce and wine. Bring to a boil and cook over low heat 5 minutes. Carefully break the eggs into the pan, cover and cook until set, about 3 minutes. Carefully put an egg on each piece of toast and cover with the sauce. Sprinkle with the parsley.

SERVES : 2–4

Fonduta

CHEESE—TRUFFLE FONDUE

1 pound fontina cheese or ¾ pound mozzarella and ¼ pound
    Bel Paese
1 cup milk
3 tablespoons butter
½ teaspoon salt
¼ teaspoon white pepper
3 egg yolks, beaten
White truffles, sliced
Sautéed sliced Italian or French bread

Fontina cheese is customarily used in Fonduta, but it isn't readily available in the United States. The combination of cheeses makes a good substitute. Dice the cheese. Soak the cheese in the milk for 30 minutes. Drain.

Combine the cheese, butter, salt and pepper in the top of a chafing dish or double boiler. Place over hot water and cook, stirring steadily, until cheese melts. Very gradually beat in the egg yolks, stirring constantly until thickened. Do not let boil. Serve in the chafing dish, or if prepared in the double boiler, pour into a hot serving dish. Sprinkle with the truffles and surround with the bread. Spear pieces of bread with a fork and dip into the *Fonduta*.

SERVES : 4–6

Carne

MEATS

Veal is unquestionably the favorite meat in Italy, and this is reflected in the provincial cuisine of northern Italy, where a menu without a veal dish is rare. It appears in many appetizing fashions—sautéed delicately in butter, with pieces of prosciutto and cheese, as veal birds, and in every possible way. When buying veal for use with the recipes in this section, if possible have the butcher cut it as thin as possible, and then pounded even thinner. For most *scallopine* recipes, leg of veal is an ideal cut. However, for a really delicious *piccata*, try to buy fillet of veal.

Beef, contrary to the above, seems to be increasing in popularity, at least in parts of northern Italy. Around Florence, of course, there is a great love for a beefsteak prepared in the local fashion, *alla Fiorentina,* over an open fire. In any event, Italian beef, lamb and pork dishes are quite unusual, and extremely delicious. None of them is difficult to prepare and the results are rewarding.

103

Cuori di Filetto "Remo"

SPLIT FILLET OF BEEF WITH
ROSEMARY AND BRANDY

1 pound fillet mignon
2 tablespoons olive oil
1 tablespoon butter
⅛ teaspoon sage
¼ teaspoon rosemary
1 bay leaf
¾ teaspoon salt
¼ teaspoon freshly ground black pepper
3 tablespoons warm brandy

Split the fillet in half lengthwise and open like a book.
Heat the oil and butter in a skillet; mix in the sage, rosemary and
bay leaf, then add the opened fillet. Cook over high heat 2 minutes on each side, or to desired degree of rareness. Season with
the salt and pepper, pour the brandy over it, and set aflame. Turn
the fillet over and serve.

SERVES : 2–3

Note: At the restaurant this dish is prepared at the table. You
can do it in a chafing dish at your table, if you like.

Cuori di Filetto Zingarella

FILLET OF BEEF WITH SHALLOT SAUCE

12-ounce fillet of beef
2 tablespoons olive oil
1 tablespoon lemon juice
¾ teaspoon salt
¼ teaspoon freshly ground black pepper
2 tablespoons butter
2 shallots, thinly sliced

Split the fillet lengthwise. Marinate in a mixture of the oil, lemon juice, salt and pepper 30 minutes, turning the meat several times.

Place the opened meat on a rack in a broiling pan. Broil 3 minutes on each side. Transfer the meat to a heated serving dish. Remove rack, and to the drippings add the butter and shallots. Place over direct high heat, bring to a boil quickly and pour over the meat.

SERVES : 2

Filetto al Vermouth

FILLET OF BEEF IN VERMOUTH

4 fillets of beef, cut 1-inch thick
2 tablespoons butter
½ cup sliced green olives
¾ teaspoon salt
¼ teaspoon freshly ground black pepper
¼ cup dry vermouth
¼ cup heavy cream

Don't have any fat wrapped around the meat. Melt the butter in a skillet; add the fillets and olives. Cook over high heat 2 minutes on each side, shaking the pan a few times. Sprinkle the meat with the salt and pepper; add the vermouth and cream. Cook over low heat 4 minutes longer, or to desired degree of rareness.

Arrange the fillets on a hot serving dish and pour the sauce over them.

SERVES : 4

Manzo con Peperonata

FILLET OF BEEF WITH PEPPER SAUCE

2 tablespoons olive oil
½ cup thinly sliced onions
1½ pounds tomatoes, diced (plum tomatoes, if available)
6 red or green peppers, cut in ½-inch slices
1½ teaspoons salt
¼ teaspoon freshly ground black pepper
1 clove garlic, minced
2 tablespoons butter
3 pounds fillet of beef, cut in ½-inch slices

Heat the oil in a skillet; sauté the onions 10 minutes, stirring frequently. Add the tomatoes; cook over low heat 10 minutes. Mix in the peppers, salt, pepper and garlic. Cook over low heat 20 minutes.

In a separate skillet, melt the butter. Brown the fillet slices on both sides over high heat. This should take only 2 to 3 minutes. Pour the sauce over the slices and cook 2 minutes longer, or to desired degree of rareness.

SERVES : 6–8

Filetto Siciliana

SAUTÉED FILLET OF BEEF IN WINE

4 fillets of beef, cut 1-inch thick
3 tablespoons butter
1 tablespoon olive oil
¼ cup sliced onions
1¼ teaspoons salt
½ teaspoon pepper
⅓ cup Marsala or sherry
¼ cup water
1 tablespoon minced parsley

Don't have any fat wrapped around the meat. Heat 2 tablespoons butter and the oil in a skillet; sauté the onions 10 minutes. Remove the onions. In the fat remaining, cook the fillets over high heat 2 minutes on each side. Stir in the remaining butter, the salt, pepper, wine, water, parsley and sautéed onions. Cook 4 minutes longer, or to desired degree of rareness. Turn the meat once.

SERVES : 4

Filetto Ripieno

STUFFED FILLET OF BEEF

6 fillets of beef, cut ¾-inch thick
6 slices prosciutto or cooked ham
6 thin slices mozzarella or Swiss cheese
1 teaspoon salt
¼ teaspoon freshly ground black pepper
⅛ cup flour
2 eggs, beaten
½ cup dry bread crumbs
5 tablespoons butter

Cut the steaks horizontally through the middle, leaving one side attached. Open like a book. Put a slice of ham and a slice of cheese on each, then close up, pressing the edges together firmly. Season with the salt and pepper, dip in the flour, the eggs, and finally the bread crumbs.

Melt the butter in a skillet; sauté the steaks 5 minutes on each side, or to desired degree of rareness.

SERVES : 6

Filetto al Pâté

FILLET OF BEEF WITH PÂTÉ

6 fillets of beef, cut 1½-inches thick
1½ teaspoons salt
½ teaspoon freshly ground black pepper
2 tablespoons olive oil
2 tablespoons butter
¼ cup Marsala or sweet sherry
4-ounce can pâté de foie gras
¼ cup warmed brandy

Season the fillets with the salt and pepper and rub with the oil. Let stand at room temperature 1 hour.

Melt the butter in a skillet; cook the fillets over high heat 1 minute on each side, or until browned. Remove. Add the wine and pâté to the skillet; cook over low heat, stirring constantly until smooth. Return the fillets; cook 2 minutes. Pour the brandy over them and set aflame; shake the pan until flames die. Transfer steaks to a serving dish and pour the sauce over them.

SERVES : 4

Bocconcini "Giovanni"

BEEF BIRDS

1½ pounds fillet of beef
1¼ teaspoons salt
½ teaspoon freshly ground black pepper
½ teaspoon oregano
⅛ teaspoon nutmeg
¼ pound prosciutto, chopped
¼ cup chopped parsley
¼ cup grated Parmesan cheese
3 tablespoons butter
1 clove garlic, minced

1 pound tomatoes, peeled and chopped
¼ pound mushrooms, sliced
1 bay leaf
½ cup dry white wine

Slice the beef as thin as possible, then pound between two sheets of waxed paper. Season one side with the salt, pepper, oregano and nutmeg. On the unseasoned side, spread a mixture of the prosciutto and parsley, then sprinkle with the cheese. Roll up into sausage shapes and fasten with toothpicks or tie with white thread.

Melt the butter in a casserole or deep skillet; brown the rolls on all sides. Mix in the garlic, then add the tomatoes, mushrooms, bay leaf and wine. Bring to a boil and cook over low heat 20 minutes. Taste for seasoning. Discard bay leaf.

SERVES : 6–8

Manzo in Salsa di Prezzemolo

BEEF WITH PARSLEY SAUCE

4 slices eye round, cut 2 inches thick (about 2 pounds)
2 tablespoons olive oil
4 anchovy fillets, chopped
1 clove garlic, minced
¼ cup chopped parsley
¾ cup dry white wine
½ teaspoon salt
¼ teaspoon freshly ground black pepper

Pound the beef with a mallet or cleaver to tenderize. Heat the oil in a skillet; brown the beef on both sides. Mix in the anchovies, garlic and parsley; cook over low heat 5 minutes. Add the wine, salt and pepper. Cover and cook over low heat 30 minutes or until meat is tender.

SERVES : 4

Bistecca alla Fiorentina

BEEFSTEAK, FLORENTINE STYLE

2 1-pound shell steaks (strip sirloin, delmonico)
¼ cup olive oil
2 tablespoons melted butter
½ teaspoon freshly ground black pepper
Salt
4 tablespoons butter
2 tablespoons lemon juice
2 tablespoons minced parsley

Buy the steak with the bone left in. Trim most of the fat. Let stand in a mixture of the oil, 2 tablespoons melted butter and pepper 30 minutes, turning the steak once or twice to coat it.

The steaks are customarily broiled over a charcoal fire, but a very hot broiler will do. Broil the steaks 5 minutes on each side, or to desired degree of rareness, turning them only once. Season with salt.

While the steaks are broiling, melt the 4 tablespoons butter. Stir in the lemon juice and parsley. Pour over the steaks.

SERVES : 2–4

Costata alla Pizzaiola

STEAK IN TOMATO SAUCE

1 2-pound delmonico (shell) steak
1 tablespoon olive oil
2 cloves garlic, minced
1 tablespoon butter
¾ cup peeled chopped tomatoes
¼ teaspoon oregano
2 tablespoons chopped parsley

1¼ teaspoons salt
¼ teaspoon black pepper

Trim most of the fat from the steak. Heat the oil in a skillet. Brown the steak in it over high heat 3 minutes on each side. Remove from pan and keep hot. Add the garlic, butter, tomatoes and oregano to the skillet. Cook over medium heat 10 minutes. Return the steak and cook over low heat 5 minutes or to desired degree of rareness. Turn the steak a few times. Sprinkle with the parsley, salt and pepper.

SERVES : 3–4

Manzo al Forno

BAKED BEEF

3 pounds bottom round
1 tablespoon olive oil
½ cup chopped onions
2 cloves garlic, minced
2 teaspoons salt
½ teaspoon black pepper
½ teaspoon rosemary
1 8-ounce can tomato sauce
½ cup beef broth
2 tablespoons minced parsley

Trim the fat off the meat. Heat the oil in a skillet; brown the meat, onions and garlic in it. Season with the salt, pepper and rosemary, then add the tomato sauce, broth and parsley. Cover and bake in a 350° oven 1½ hours or until meat is tender.

SERVES : 6–8

Stufato di Manzo

BEEF WITH WHITE WINE

3 pounds eye round, cross rib, etc.
4 tablespoons butter
3 cups thinly sliced onions
1½ cups peeled diced tomatoes
¾ cup sliced carrots
¼ cup sliced celery
2 teaspoons salt
½ teaspoon freshly ground black pepper
½ teaspoon basil
1 cup dry white wine

Rinse the meat and pat dry. Melt the butter in a Dutch oven or heavy skillet; sauté the onions until soft and yellow. Add the meat and brown it on all sides. Add the tomatoes, carrots, celery, salt, pepper, basil and wine. Bring to a boil, cover and cook over low heat 2 hours or until the meat is tender. Slice the meat and serve with the gravy.

SERVES : 6–8

Costata di Manzo al Vino Rosso

MARINATED ROAST BEEF

2 or 3 rib roast
3 cups dry red wine
¾ cup sliced onions
½ cup sliced carrots
2 cloves garlic, minced
2 bay leaves
½ teaspoon freshly ground black pepper
2½ teaspoons salt

Have the bones cut down very short and the meat trimmed and weighed. Put the meat in a bowl (not metal). Pour the wine over it, and add the onions, carrots, garlic, bay leaves and pepper. Marinate in the refrigerator 24 hours, basting and turning the meat several times.

Drain (reserve marinade) and dry the meat with paper towels; rub with the salt. Place in a shallow roasting pan; roast in a 450° oven 20 minutes. Meanwhile, cook the marinade until reduced to half. Pour over the meat; roast 15 minutes a pound, basting frequently.

SERVES : 4–8

Manzo Ripieno

STUFFED BEEF

1 flank steak
2 slices white bread
½ cup water
¼ pound chicken livers, diced
¾ cup chopped onions
¼ cup chopped celery
¼ cup minced parsley
¼ cup grated Parmesan cheese
¼ pound cooked ham, cut julienne
1 egg, beaten
2½ teaspoons salt
¼ teaspoon freshly ground black pepper
¼ teaspoon oregano
3 tablespoons olive oil
2 cups water

Have the steak pounded very thin. Soak the bread in the water 10 minutes; drain and mash smooth. Combine with the livers, onions, celery, parsley, cheese, ham, egg, 1 teaspoon salt,

¼ teaspoon pepper and ¼ teaspoon oregano. Spread on the steak; roll up and tie with string. Heat the oil in a Dutch oven or heavy deep skillet; brown the roll in it. Sprinkle with the remaining salt, pepper and oregano; add the water. Cover and cook over low heat 2 hours or until tender. Serve warm (meat should stand at room temperature 20 minutes for easier slicing) or cold.

SERVES : 4–6

Manzo Brasato

BRAISED BEEF IN RED WINE

4 pounds eye round, cross rib or rump of beef
4 tablespoons olive oil
1 tablespoon butter
2 cups dry red wine
1½ cups chopped onions
½ cup grated carrots
½ cup diced celery
2 cloves garlic, minced
2 teaspoons salt
½ teaspoon freshly ground black pepper
½ teaspoon rosemary
1 bay leaf
Dash ground cloves
1½ cups diced tomatoes

Have the beef larded or do it yourself. Put all the ingredients in a Dutch oven or heavy saucepan. Cover tightly; bring to a boil and cook over low heat 2½ hours or until tender. Discard bay leaf. Transfer the meat to a baking pan; purée the vegetables in an electric blender or force through a sieve. Pour over the meat. Bake in a 450° oven 15 minutes.

SERVES : 6–8

Bollito Misto

BOILED MIXED MEATS

A variety of meats are used in the traditional Bollito Misto. It is best to prepare this dish for at least 8 people, so that enough different meats can be included. However, at least 2 different meats and a sausage should be used.

Here is a typical combination:

A small smoked tongue
2 whole onions
2 carrots
2 stalks celery
4 sprigs parsley
An eye round of beef
A piece of rolled veal
A small fowl
Italian pork sausages
½ teaspoon freshly ground black pepper

Cover the tongue with water in a very large kettle, bring to a boil and drain. Add fresh boiling water to cover, and the onions, carrots, celery and parsley. Bring to a boil and cook over low heat 1 hour. Skim the top. Add the beef and veal, cook 1 hour. Skim the top. Add the chicken, sausages and pepper. Cook 1 hour. Taste for seasoning, adding salt if necessary. Arrange the meats on a serving dish and serve with Salsa Piccante, mustard or Tomato Sauce. Strain the broth and use for other purposes.

Abbacchio al Forno

BAKED LEG OF LAMB

4-pound leg of baby lamb
1 tablespoon salt

1 teaspoon freshly ground black pepper
5 cloves garlic, minced
2 teaspoons rosemary
½ cup melted butter

Rub the lamb with a mixture of the salt, pepper, garlic and rosemary. Let stand 1 hour. Place on a rack in a roasting pan. Roast in a 375° oven 1 hour or until meat is tender but still pink. Baste frequently with melted butter.

SERVES : 6

Abbacchio Marinato

MARINATED ROAST LAMB

4 to 5-pound leg of lamb
1 tablespoon salt
¾ teaspoon freshly ground black pepper
1 teaspoon rosemary
½ cup olive oil
⅛ cup wine vinegar
1 cup dry red wine

Remove the fell (skin) of the lamb and trim the fat. Prick the lamb in several places, then rub with the salt, pepper and rosemary. Place in a bowl, and pour over the oil mixed with the vinegar and wine. Marinate in the refrigerator overnight, basting frequently with the marinade.

Drain (reserving the marinade) and place in a roasting pan. Roast in a 350° oven 15 minutes a pound, or to desired degree of rareness. (In Italy, the lamb is served pink.) Add the marinade after 30 minutes roasting time, and baste frequently thereafter.

SERVES : 6–8

Costolette di Agnello al Cartoccio

LAMB CUTLETS IN PAPER

4 lamb cutlets, cut ¼-inch thick
2 teaspoons salt
¼ teaspoon freshly ground black pepper
3 dried mushrooms
2 tablespoons olive oil
¾ cup chopped onions
⅛ teaspoon nutmeg
2 tablespoons melted butter
8 slices prosciutto or cooked ham

Season the lamb cutlets with 1½ teaspoons salt and the pepper. Soak the mushrooms in warm water 10 minutes. Drain and chop. Heat the oil in a skillet; sauté the onions 5 minutes; mix in the mushrooms, nutmeg and remaining salt. Cook over very low heat 10 minutes. Cool 5 minutes.

Cut 4 pieces of parchment paper or aluminum foil large enough to completely cover the lamb. Brush with butter, place a slice of ham on it, spread with onion mixture, place a cutlet over it and cover with a slice of ham. Bring up the edges of the paper and seal the edges. Place on a baking sheet. Bake in a 350° oven 45 minutes. Slit paper, and serve directly from it.

SERVES : 4

Abbacchio alla Romana

LAMB WITH ARTICHOKES AND EGG SAUCE

2 tablespoons butter
3 pounds shoulder of lamb, cut in 1-inch cubes
2½ teaspoons salt
¼ teaspoon freshly ground black pepper
½ cup dry white wine

½ cup beef broth
1 package frozen artichoke hearts, cooked and drained
4 eggs
½ cup grated Parmesan cheese
2 tablespoons minced parsley

Melt the butter in a casserole or deep skillet with oven-proof handle. Brown the lamb in it. Season with 2 teaspoons salt and the pepper. Add the wine; cook until evaporated. Mix in the broth; cover and bake in a 350° oven 45 minutes, adding the artichokes after 35 minutes.

Beat the eggs, remaining salt, the cheese and parsley. Pour over the lamb and artichokes. Bake uncovered, 10 minutes longer.

SERVES : 6

Abbacchio alla Ciociara

BRAISED LAMB WITH HAM

3 pounds shoulder of lamb, cut in 1-inch cubes
2 teaspoons salt
½ teaspoon freshly ground black pepper
2 tablespoons butter
¼ pound prosciutto or cooked ham, cut julienne
½ cup brandy
¼ teaspoon rosemary
1 clove garlic, minced

Season the lamb with the salt and pepper. Melt the butter in a deep skillet or casserole; brown the lamb in it. Add the ham; cook 5 minutes. Mix in the brandy, rosemary and garlic; cover and cook over low heat 1 hour, or until lamb is tender. Watch carefully and add a little boiling water if necessary to keep from burning. There should be a very little gravy when meat is finished.

SERVES : 6

Scaloppine "Chic Martini"

VEAL AND ARTICHOKES

Artichokes:

4 small artichokes
½ cup olive oil
½ cup water
1 clove garlic, minced
¼ cup chopped parsley
½ teaspoon freshly ground black pepper

Wash the artichokes, cut off the stems and cut in half lengthwise. Arrange in a shallow baking pan, cut side up, and cover with a mixture of the oil, water, garlic, parsley and pepper. Bake in a preheated 450° oven 25 minutes or until the liquid is evaporated. While the artichokes are baking, prepare the veal.

Veal:

1 pound veal scallops
¼ cup flour
2 eggs
1 teaspoon salt
¼ teaspoon freshly ground black pepper
½ cup grated Parmesan cheese
3 tablespoons olive oil
1 tablespoon butter
Lemon wedges

Have the veal pounded very thin. Dip the slices in the flour, then in the eggs beaten with the salt and pepper, and finally the cheese. There should be a thick coating on each slice.

Heat the oil and butter in a large skillet; sauté the veal in it over low heat until browned on both sides. Arrange on a heated serving dish, with the artichokes and lemon wedges around it.

SERVES : 4

Scaloppine di Vitello Zingarella

SCALOPPINE OF VEAL ZINGARELLA

1 pound veal scallops
¼ cup flour
2 tablespoons olive oil
½ cup dry white wine
4 red or green peppers, sliced thin and lightly sautéed
1 8-ounce can tomatoes, drained
1½ teaspoons salt
¼ teaspoon freshly ground black pepper
⅛ teaspoon oregano

Have the veal pounded very thin. Dip in the flour. Heat the oil in a skillet; brown the veal on both sides. Add the wine; cook over medium heat until evaporated. Add the peppers, tomatoes, salt, pepper and oregano. Cook over low heat 20 minutes.

SERVES : 4

Piccata di Vitello

VEAL IN LEMON SAUCE

1 pound veal scallops
¼ cup flour
1½ teaspoons salt
¼ teaspoon freshly ground black pepper
2 tablespoons olive oil
2 tablespoons butter
2 tablespoons lemon juice
2 tablespoons minced parsley

Have the veal pounded very thin. Dip the slices in a mixture of the flour, salt, and pepper.

Heat the oil and butter in a large skillet until it sizzles.

Brown the veal in it on both sides. Have the veal flat, in a single layer. When browned and tender, remove the veal. Pour off the fat, and add the lemon juice and parsley. Return the veal and heat, stirring well to coat veal with lemon juice and parsley.

SERVES : 4

Scaloppine di Vitello al Prosciutto

VEAL AND HAM CUTLETS

6 very thin veal cutlets
1¼ teaspoons salt
¼ teaspoon freshly ground black pepper
4 tablespoons butter
6 slices prosciutto or cooked ham
1 cup sliced sautéed mushrooms
1½ cups cooked green peas
¾ cup dry white wine
2 tablespoons minced parsley

Pound the veal very thin; season with the salt and pepper. Melt the butter in a skillet; brown the veal on both sides. Place a slice of ham on each cutlet; add the mushrooms, peas and wine. Cook over low heat 10 minutes. Sprinkle with the parsley.

SERVES : 6

Bracioline di Vitello Ripieno

STUFFED VEAL ROLLS

8 veal scallops (1 pound)
1¼ teaspoons salt
¼ teaspoon freshly ground black pepper

¾ cup finely chopped ham
¼ cup chopped mushrooms
2 tablespoons grated Parmesan cheese
1 tablespoon brandy
¼ cup flour
4 tablespoons butter
½ cup dry white wine

Pound the scallops as thin as possible. Season one side with
the salt and pepper. Mix together the ham, mushrooms, cheese
and brandy. Spread 2 heaping tablespoons on the unseasoned
side of the veal. Roll up and tie with thread or fasten with toothpicks. Roll in the flour.

Melt the butter in a skillet; brown the rolls in it. Add the
wine; cover and cook over low heat 15 minutes or until the rolls
are tender and the wine is almost absorbed.

SERVES : 4

Costolette di Vitello al Cartoccio

VEAL CHOPS IN PAPER

2 tablespoons butter
¼ pound mushrooms, thinly sliced
1 cup peeled diced tomatoes
¼ cup julienne-cut ham
¼ cup dry white wine
2½ teaspoons salt
½ teaspoon freshly ground black pepper
6 veal chops, cut 1-inch thick
3 tablespoons olive oil
2 tablespoons minced parsley

Melt the butter in a saucepan; sauté the mushrooms 3 minutes. Add the tomatoes, ham, wine, 1 teaspoon salt and ¼ teaspoon
pepper. Bring to a boil and cook over low heat 10 minutes.

Season the chops with the remaining salt and pepper. Heat 2 tablespoons oil in a skillet; brown the chops in it on both sides. Cut 6 pieces of parchment paper or aluminum foil large enough to completely cover the chops. Brush with remaining oil. Place a chop in the center of each and cover with the sauce. Sprinkle with the parsley. Fold over the paper, sealing the edges well. Place on a baking sheet; bake in a 375° oven 15 minutes or until chops are tender. Serve in the paper, with the top rolled back.

SERVES : 6

Costolette di Vitello Ripiene

BREADED STUFFED VEAL CHOPS

4 veal chops, cut ¾-inch thick
4 slices prosciutto ham
4 thin slices mozzarella cheese
¼ cup flour
1½ teaspoons salt
¼ teaspoon pepper
1 egg, beaten
½ cup dry bread crumbs
4 tablespoons butter

Split the chops, but leave one side connected. Open the chops (like a book) and pound each side as thin as possible. Place a slice of ham and cheese on each. Close the chops (don't let the cheese come too close to the edges), moisten the edges and press together. Dip lightly in the flour mixed with the salt and pepper, then in the egg, and finally in the bread crumbs.

Melt the butter in a skillet; sauté the chops 10 minutes on each side or until tender and browned. Serve with lemon wedges.

SERVES : 4

Costolette di Vitello Valdostana

STUFFED VEAL CHOPS

6 veal chops, cut 1-inch thick
6 slices prosciutto ham
6 slices mozzarella cheese
1 tablespoon minced truffles
½ teaspoon salt
½ teaspoon freshly ground black pepper
¼ cup flour
6 tablespoons butter
½ cup dry white wine
¼ teaspoon rosemary

Have a pocket made in each chop by cutting through the middle horizontally, so that each opens like a book. Pound the chops flat lightly. Place a slice of prosciutto and cheese on one side of each, sprinkle with the truffles, and close the chops. Squeeze the edges closed. Season with the salt and pepper and dip in the flour.

Heat the butter in a skillet; sauté the veal until browned on both sides. Add the wine and rosemary; cover and cook over low heat 25 minutes or until tender.

SERVES : 6

Uccelletti Scappati

VEAL BIRDS

14 veal scallops
1 clove garlic, minced
¼ cup finely chopped parsley
2 tablespoons dry white wine
⅛ teaspoon nutmeg
2 teaspoons salt

½ teaspoon freshly ground black pepper
⅛ cup flour
6 tablespoons butter
¼ teaspoon sage

Grind 2 veal scallops in a food chopper. Mix in the garlic, parsley, wine, nutmeg, ¾ teaspoon salt and ¼ teaspoon pepper. Spread some of the mixture on each of the 12 scallops, roll up and tie with white thread.

Mix the flour with the remaining salt and pepper; dip the rolls in the mixture. Melt the butter in a skillet; add the sage and rolls. Sauté 20 minutes or until browned on all sides and tender.

SERVES : 6

Saltimbocca alla Romana

VEAL–HAM MEDALLIONS

12 veal scallops
1¼ teaspoons salt
¼ teaspoon freshly ground black pepper
12 fresh sage leaves or ½ teaspoon dried sage
12 slices prosciutto ham
4 tablespoons butter
¼ cup Marsala

Have the veal pounded as thin as possible and cut into 5-inch squares; season with the salt and pepper. Put a sage leaf or a little dried sage on each; cover with a slice of ham (cut to same size) over each slice of veal. Fasten with toothpicks.

Melt the butter in a skillet; brown the medallions in it over high heat on both sides. Add the wine; cook over low heat 5 minutes or until the veal is tender. Place on a heated serving dish, ham side up. Remove toothpicks. Pour gravy over all.

SERVES : 6

Costolette alla Bolognese

VEAL CUTLETS, BOLOGNA STYLE

4 veal chops
1¼ teaspoons salt
¼ teaspoon freshly ground black pepper
1 egg, beaten
½ cup dry bread crumbs
2 tablespoons butter
8 slices cooked ham
8 slices fontina or Gruyère cheese

Have the veal pounded very thin. Season with the salt and pepper, dip in the egg, and then the bread crumbs.

Melt the butter in a skillet; brown the veal on under side. Turn over and place a slice of ham and cheese, cut to fit veal, on top. Cover skillet and cook until veal is tender and cheese melted.

SERVES : 4

Spezzatino di Vitello in Umido

VEAL STEW

3 pound veal, cut in 1½-inch cubes
¼ cup flour
2 teaspoons salt
¼ teaspoon freshly ground black pepper
½ teaspoon thyme
2 tablespoons olive oil
4 tablespoons butter
½ cup chopped onions
½ cup Marsala or sweet sherry
2 teaspoons tomato paste
2 tablespoons heavy cream

1 cup sautéed sliced mushrooms
2 cups cooked green peas

Toss the veal in a mixture of the flour, salt, pepper, and thyme. Heat the oil and 2 tablespoons butter in a Dutch oven or heavy saucepan; brown the veal and onions in it. Add the wine and tomato paste; cover and cook over low heat 45 minutes or until veal is tender. Add the remaining butter, the cream, mushrooms and peas; cook 5 minutes longer.

SERVES : 6

Scaloppine al Fegato

VEAL WITH CHICKEN LIVERS

8 veal scallops (1 pound)
¼ cup flour
2½ teaspoons salt
¾ teaspoon freshly ground black pepper
¼ cup olive oil
½ pound chicken livers, diced
½ cup peeled chopped tomatoes
¼ teaspoon thyme

Have the veal pounded as thin as possible; dip in a mixture of the flour and half the salt and pepper.

Heat the oil in a skillet; brown 1 minute on each side over high heat. Add the livers; cook over high heat 3 minutes. Add the tomatoes, thyme and the remaining salt and pepper; cook over medium heat 5 minutes longer. Serve with *Risotto* (see recipe p. 87).

SERVES : 4

Scaloppine con Carciofi

VEAL AND ARTICHOKES CASSEROLE

1 package frozen artichoke hearts, thawed
3 tablespoons butter
2½ teaspoons salt
12 veal scallops
1 egg, beaten
¼ cup flour
¼ teaspoon freshly ground pepper
3 tablespoons olive oil
¼ cup beef broth
⅛ cup grated Parmesan cheese

Sauté the artichokes in the butter 5 minutes. Season with 1 teaspoon salt. Dip the veal scallops in the egg, then in a mixture of the flour, pepper and remaining salt.

Heat the oil in a skillet; brown the veal on both sides. Arrange in a greased shallow casserole (or use skillet, with ovenproof handle). Add the broth, cover veal with artichokes and sprinkle with the cheese. Bake in a 375° oven 10 minutes or until browned.

SERVES : 6

Vitello alla Paesana

BREAST OF VEAL, COUNTRY STYLE

1 breast of veal
2 tablespoons olive oil
2 tablespoons butter
¾ cup chopped onions
¼ cup chopped celery
2 cups peeled cubed tomatoes
2 teaspoons salt
½ teaspoon freshly ground black pepper

½ teaspoon basil
½ cup hot beef broth
1 package frozen peas and carrots, thawed
2 tablespoons minced parsley

Have the veal cut up into serving-sized pieces, bone and all. Heat the oil and butter in a Dutch oven or heavy casserole; sauté the onions and celery 5 minutes. Add the veal; cook until browned. Add the tomatoes, salt, pepper and basil. Cover and bake in a 300° oven 1¼ hours, adding the broth from time to time. Skim the fat. Add the peas and carrots; recover and bake 15 minutes longer. Sprinkle with the parsley.

SERVES : 4–5

Arrosto Semplice di Vitello

PAN-ROASTED VEAL

3-pound rolled veal roast
2 teaspoons salt
½ teaspoon freshly ground black pepper
½ teaspoon rosemary
3 tablespoons butter
¼ cup brandy
¼ cup milk
2 tablespoons minced parsley

Rub the meat with a mixture of the salt, pepper and rosemary. Melt the butter in a Dutch oven or heavy saucepan. Brown the meat in it on all sides, being careful not to prick it. Add the brandy; cover and cook over low heat 1½ hours or until tender; add the milk from time to time. Slice thin, and serve with the pan juices, skimmed of fat, and mixed with the parsley.

SERVES : 4–6

Arancine Saporite nel Pomodoro

SMALL VEAL BALLS IN TOMATO SAUCE

1 pound ground veal
½ pound mortadella or bologna, ground
¼ cup Parmesan cheese
2 eggs
2 teaspoons salt
½ teaspoon freshly ground black pepper
⅛ teaspoon nutmeg
½ cup flour
4 tablespoons olive oil
1 cup chopped onions
1 carrot, grated
1 pound tomatoes, cubed
2 tablespoons butter
1 clove garlic, minced

Mix together the veal, mortadella, cheese, eggs, 1 teaspoon salt, ¼ teaspoon pepper and the nutmeg. Shape into walnut-sized balls and roll in the flour. Chill while preparing the sauce.

Heat half the oil in a saucepan; sauté the onions and carrot 10 minutes. Add the tomatoes and the remaining salt and pepper. Cook over low heat 30 minutes. Purée in an electric blender or force through a sieve.

Heat the butter and remaining oil in a skillet. Add the garlic and veal balls; brown balls on all sides. Add the tomato sauce and cook over low heat 20 minutes.

SERVES : 4–6, or serve as a hot hors d'oeuvre.

Osso Buco alla Milanese

BRAISED VEAL KNUCKLE

3 pounds veal shin
¼ cup flour

2 tablespoons olive oil
2 tablespoons butter
2 teaspoons salt
½ teaspoon freshly ground black pepper
¼ teaspoon rosemary
¾ cup chopped onions
¼ cup grated carrots
1 stalk celery, chopped
1 cup dry white wine
1 tablespoon tomato paste
½ cup water
2 tablespoons grated lemon rind
1 clove garlic, minced
2 tablespoons minced parsley

Have the veal shins sawed into 2-inch pieces—be sure the bones are well covered with meat. Roll lightly in the flour.

Heat the oil and butter in a Dutch oven or heavy saucepan; brown the shins in it. Sprinkle with the salt, pepper and rosemary; add the onions, carrots and celery. Cook 5 minutes. Add the wine. Cook until evaporated. Mix in the tomato paste and water. Cover and cook over low heat 2 hours, or until tender. Add small amounts of boiling water from time to time if necessary. Mix together the lemon rind, garlic and parsley; stir into the gravy. Recover and cook 5 minutes longer. Serve with *Risotto* (see recipe, p. 87) or boiled rice.

SERVES : 6

Vitello Tonnato alla Casalinga

VEAL IN TUNA FISH SAUCE, HOME STYLE

¼ cup olive oil
4 pounds rolled veal
1 cup sliced onions
1 7¾-ounce can tuna fish, flaked

1 can anchovy fillets, minced
2 cloves garlic
2 bay leaves
½ teaspoon thyme
2 cups dry white wine
1 cup chicken broth
Rind of 1 orange
Rind of 1 lemon
½ teaspoon freshly ground black pepper
2 teaspoons salt
½ cup mayonnaise

Heat the oil in a Dutch oven or heavy saucepan; brown the veal in it. Pour off the fat. Add the onions, undrained flaked tuna fish, anchovies, garlic, bay leaves, thyme, wine, broth, orange rind, lemon rind, pepper and salt. Cover and cook over low heat 2 hours or until tender. Let cool in the gravy. Remove the veal; discard the bay leaves, orange and lemon rind. Purée the gravy in an electric blender or force through a sieve. Measure 3 cups gravy and gradually mix into the mayonnaise. Slice the veal and pour gravy over it. Let marinate in the refrigerator 4 hours before serving. Garnish with capers.

SERVES : 6–8

Arista Fiorentina

ROAST PORK, FLORENCE STYLE

8-rib loin of pork
3 cloves garlic, cut in slivers
½ teaspoon rosemary
2½ teaspoons salt
¾ teaspoon freshly ground black pepper
2 cups dry white wine

Trim the fat off the pork. Make a few incisions in the pork. Dip the garlic slivers in the rosemary and insert in the cuts. Rub the pork with the salt and pepper. Place in a shallow roasting pan. Roast in a 400° oven 45 minutes. Pour off the fat. Reduce heat to 350°, pour the wine over the pork and roast 2¼ hours longer, basting it every half hour. Serve hot or cold.

SERVES : 4–6

Costolette di Maiale Milanese

BREADED PORK CHOPS

4 pork chops, cut 1-inch thick
1 egg, beaten
1½ teaspoons salt
¼ teaspoon freshly ground black pepper
⅓ cup grated Parmesan cheese
⅓ cup dry bread crumbs
2 tablespoons olive oil
2 tablespoons butter

Trim the fat off the chops. Dip in a mixture of the egg, salt and pepper, then in the cheese mixed with the bread crumbs.

Heat the olive oil and butter in a skillet (with ovenproof handle). Brown the chops on both sides over direct low heat, then bake in a 350° oven 35 minutes or until tender and no pink remains. Turn the chops twice.

SERVES : 4

Costolette di Maiale Pizzaiola

PORK CHOPS PIZZAIOLA

6 loin or rib pork chops, cut ¾-inch thick
2 teaspoons salt
½ teaspoon freshly ground black pepper

2 cloves garlic, minced
2 tablespoons olive oil
½ cup canned tomato sauce
¼ cup dry red wine
¼ teaspoon oregano
2 green peppers, cut julienne
½ pound mushrooms, sliced
3 Italian sausages, sliced

Rub the chops with a mixture of the salt, pepper and garlic. Heat the oil in a skillet; brown the chops on both sides. Add the tomato sauce, wine, oregano, green peppers and mushrooms. Cover and cook over low heat 25 minutes or until pork is tender. Taste for seasoning.

Brown the sausages, drain, and add to skillet 10 minutes before end of cooking time.

SERVES : 6

Braciole di Maiale Piccanti

BREADED PORK CHOPS WITH CAPER SAUCE

4 pork chops, cut ¾-inch thick
1 egg
1 teaspoon salt
¼ teaspoon freshly ground black pepper
½ cup dry bread crumbs
¼ cup vegetable oil
2 tablespoons butter
2 tablespoons chopped capers
⅓ cup beef broth

Trim the fat off the chops; dip chops in the egg, beaten with the salt and pepper, then coat with the bread crumbs.

Heat the oil in a skillet; cook the chops in it 15 minutes on each side. Pour off the oil and add the butter, capers and broth. Cook 10 minutes longer.

SERVES : 4

Bracioline di Maiale alla Toscana

BRAISED PORK CHOPS

6 pork chops, cut ¾-inch thick
2 teaspoons salt
½ teaspoon freshly ground black pepper
⅛ teaspoon fennel seeds
2 tablespoons olive oil
1 clove garlic, minced
½ cup boiling water

Trim the fat off the chops; season with the salt, pepper and fennel.

Heat the oil in a skillet, brown the chops and garlic over high heat. Pour off the fat and add the water. Cover and cook over low heat 30 minutes.

SERVES : 6

Involtini di Maiale

PORK ROLLS

6 slices of pork, cut ¼-inch thick
2 teaspoons salt
½ teaspoon freshly ground black pepper
¼ pound ground pork
¼ pound chicken livers, ground
1 tablespoon olive oil
2 tablespoons minced onion

¼ teaspoon rosemary
¼ teaspoon oregano
1 tablespoon minced parsley
2 eggs, beaten
2 tablespoons butter
¾ cup beef broth

Pound the pork between two pieces of waxed paper until very thin. The pieces should be about 4-inches square. Season with 1½ teaspoons salt and ¼ teaspoon pepper.

Mix together the ground pork, the livers, oil, onion, rosemary, oregano, parsley and the remaining salt and pepper. Beat in the eggs. Divide the filling among the pork slices and roll up; fasten them with toothpicks or tie with white thread.

Melt the butter in a skillet; brown the rolls in it. Add half the broth; cover and cook over low heat 45 minutes, adding the remaining broth from time to time.

SERVES : 6

Spezzato di Maiale alla Carbonara

MINCED PORK AND ONIONS

3 tablespoons butter
4 cups chopped onions
1½ teaspoons salt
2 pounds pork, cut in very small pieces
¼ teaspoon freshly ground black pepper
1 cup dry white wine
1 tablespoon flour
¾ cup beef broth

Melt 2 tablespoons butter in a skillet; mix in the onions and half the salt. Cook over low heat 20 minutes, stirring frequently. Spread half the onions on the bottom of a baking dish.

Season the pork with the pepper and remaining salt. Spread over the onions and cover pork with the remaining onions. Pour the wine into the dish.

Melt the remaining butter in a saucepan; blend in the flour. Gradually add the broth, stirring steadily to the boiling point. Cook over low heat 5 minutes, then pour over the onions. Bake in a 350° oven 1¼ hours. Serve with boiled potatoes.

SERVES : 4–6

Torta di Patate e Prosciutto

POTATO—HAM PIE

1½ pounds potatoes
2 teaspoons salt
¼ teaspoon white pepper
⅛ teaspoon nutmeg
6 tablespoons butter
¼ cup dry bread crumbs
¼ pound Bel Paese or Swiss cheese, cut julienne
½ pound prosciutto or cooked ham, cut julienne
4 hard-cooked eggs, quartered

Cook the unpeeled potatoes until tender. Drain, peel and mash smooth with the salt, pepper, nutmeg and 2 tablespoons butter.

Spread 2 tablespoons butter in a 9-inch pie plate. Dust with half the bread crumbs, then cover with half the potatoes. Arrange the cheese, ham and eggs over it, then cover with the remaining potatoes. Sprinkle with the remaining bread crumbs and dot with the remaining butter. Bake in a preheated 400° oven 25 minutes or until browned. Cut into wedges.

SERVES : 4–6 as a luncheon dish.

Cervello all'Aceto

BRAINS IN BROWN BUTTER

1½ pounds calf's brains
1 carrot, quartered
1 stalk celery, sliced
¼ teaspoon thyme
¼ teaspoon oregano
1½ teaspoons salt
3 cups water
3 tablespoons butter
2 tablespoons vinegar
2 tablespoons minced parsley
1 tablespoon capers

Wash the brains, remove the veins and connective tissues, and soak in cold water 30 minutes. Drain. Combine in a saucepan with the carrot, celery, thyme, oregano, salt and water. Bring to a boil and cook over low heat 25 minutes. Drain well and place on a hot serving dish.

Melt the butter until browned. Mix in the vinegar and parsley. Pour over the brains and sprinkle with the capers.

SERVES : 4

Cervello alla Milanese

BREADED BRAINS, MILAN FASHION

1½ pounds calf's brains
¼ cup flour
1 egg
1 teaspoon salt
⅓ cup dry bread crumbs
3 tablespoons butter

Wash the brains, remove the veins and connective tissues, and soak in cold water 30 minutes. Drain and dry, then cut in ½-inch cubes. Dip the pieces in the flour, then in the egg beaten with the salt, and finally roll in the bread crumbs.

Melt the butter in a skillet; brown the brains in it on all sides. Garnish with lemon wedges.

SERVES : 4–6

Crocchette di Cervella

BRAIN CROQUETTES

1 pound calf's brains
1 tablespoon vinegar
1¼ teaspoons salt
¼ teaspoon white pepper
½ cup chopped sautéed onions
1 egg, beaten
¼ cup flour
4 tablespoons butter

Wash the brains, cover with cold water and let stand 10 minutes. Drain, add fresh water to cover, and the vinegar. Bring to a boil and cook over low heat 15 minutes. Drain and cover with cold water; let stand 15 minutes. Drain, remove the membranes and mash the brains to a paste. Mix in the salt, pepper and onions. Chill. Form into 8 croquettes; dip in the egg, then in the flour.

Melt the butter in a skillet; brown the croquettes on both sides. Serve with lemon wedges.

SERVES : 4

Fegato di Vitello alla Milanese

BREADED CALF'S LIVER

1 pound calf's liver, sliced ¼-inch thick
2 tablespoons lemon juice
½ teaspoon freshly ground black pepper
1 egg
1 tablespoon water
½ cup dry bread crumbs
1¼ teaspoons salt
4 tablespoons butter
2 tablespoons minced parsley

Wash and dry the liver; rub with the lemon juice and pepper. Let stand in the refrigerator 1 hour.

Beat the egg and water together; dip the liver slices in it and then in the bread crumbs mixed with the salt. Melt the butter in a skillet; sauté the liver 3 minutes on each side or to desired degree of rareness. Remove the liver to a heated serving dish. Stir the parsley into the skillet; pour over the liver. If you like, serve the liver on a slice of sautéed bread.

SERVES : 4

Fegato di Vitello alla Veneziana

CALF'S LIVER, VENETIAN STYLE

1 pound calf's liver
¼ pound butter
2 cups thinly sliced onions
1 teaspoon salt
¼ teaspoon freshly ground black pepper
¼ cup dry white wine
2 tablespoons minced parsley

Cut the liver in paper-thin slices and then into strips about 1 inch by 2 inches.

Melt the butter in a skillet; add the onions. Cover and cook over very low heat 15 minutes or until lightly browned and soft. Add the liver and cook over high heat 3 minutes, stirring almost constantly. Season with the salt and pepper. Transfer to a hot platter. Add the wine and parsley to the skillet; bring to a boil and pour over the liver.

SERVES : 4

Fegatini di Pollo

CHICKEN LIVERS IN WINE SAUCE

1 pound chicken livers
4 slices bacon, diced
4 tablespoons butter
1¼ teaspoons salt
¼ teaspoon freshly ground black pepper
⅛ teaspoon sage
½ cup Marsala or sweet sherry

Wash the livers and remove any discolored spots; cut each half in two.

In a skillet, lightly brown the bacon; pour off the fat. Add the butter to the skillet, and when melted, the livers. Sauté 2 minutes; season with the salt, pepper and sage. Sauté 2 minutes longer. Remove and keep hot.

Stir the wine into the skillet, scraping the bottom of browned particles. Cook over medium heat 1 minute. Pour over the livers. The livers may be served on sautéed bread, if you like.

SERVES : 4

Animelle alla Ciociara

SWEETBREADS, HAM AND MUSHROOMS

3 pair sweetbreads
1 tablespoon vinegar
2 teaspoons salt
¼ cup flour
4 tablespoons olive oil
4 tablespoons butter
¼ teaspoon white pepper
1 cup sliced sautéed mushrooms
½ cup julienne-cut prosciutto or cooked ham
¾ cup dry white wine

Wash the sweetbreads, cover with cold water and let soak 1 hour. Drain, add fresh water to cover, the vinegar and 1 teaspoon salt. Bring to a boil and cook over low heat 5 minutes. Drain, cover with cold water and let stand 20 minutes. Drain, remove the membranes and tubes, but leave each half whole. Dry, then dip lightly in the flour.

Heat the oil in a skillet; brown the sweetbreads in it. Pour off the oil. Add the butter, pepper, mushrooms, ham, wine and the remaining salt. Bring to a boil and cook over low heat 10 minutes.

SERVES : 6

Rognoni di Vitello al Marsala

KIDNEYS IN MARSALA

1 pound veal kidneys
3 cups boiling water
2 tablespoons lemon juice
4 tablespoons butter
1¼ teaspoons salt
¼ teaspoon freshly ground black pepper

1 teaspoon grated lemon rind
½ cup Marsala or sweet sherry
3 tablespoons minced parsley

Wash the kidneys, cut in half and remove the core. Soak
in the boiling water mixed with the lemon juice for 3 minutes.
Drain, then slice thin.

Melt the butter in a skillet; sauté the kidneys 5 minutes. Season
with the salt, pepper and lemon rind and add the wine. Cook over
medium heat 5 minutes. Sprinkle with the parsley.

SERVES : 4

Rognoni al Vino Bianco

KIDNEYS IN WHITE WINE

1 pound veal kidneys
Boiling water
½ cup warm dry white wine
4 tablespoons butter
2 cups thinly sliced onions
1½ teaspoons salt
¼ teaspoon freshly ground black pepper

Wash the kidneys, cut in half and remove the core. Soak
in boiling water 5 minutes. Drain, dry and slice. Marinate in
the wine 1 hour. Drain and dry, reserving the marinade.

While the kidneys are marinating, prepare the onions. Melt
the butter in a skillet; sauté the onions over very low heat until
soft and yellow. Sprinkle with the salt and pepper. Add the kidneys and ¼ cup of the reserved marinade; cover and cook over low
heat 15 minutes, adding the remaining marinade after 10 minutes.
Serve with sautéed Italian or French bread.

SERVES : 4

Trippa alla Fiorentina

TRIPE IN MEAT SAUCE

2 pounds tripe
2 tablespoons butter
¾ cup chopped onions
¼ cup grated carrots
½ pound beef
½ cup dry white wine
¾ cup peeled chopped tomatoes
¼ cup water
2 teaspoons salt
½ teaspoon freshly ground black pepper
½ teaspoon marjoram
½ cup grated Parmesan cheese

Wash the tripe, cover with water and bring to a boil; cook over low heat 1 hour. Drain, cool and cut into 2-inch long, ½-inch wide strips. Prepare the sauce while the tripe is cooking.

Melt the butter in a saucepan; brown the onions, carrots and beef in it. Add the wine, tomatoes, water, salt and pepper; bring to a boil, cover and cook over low heat 1 hour. Add the marjoram and tripe; recover and cook 1 hour longer. Remove the beef; mix the cheese into the tripe.

SERVES : 6–8

Code di Bue alla Romagnola

BRAISED OXTAILS

2 oxtails
1 carrot
3 sprigs parsley
3 teaspoons salt
2 tablespoons butter

¼ cup chopped onions
¾ cup diced celery
¼ pound ham, cut julienne
¾ cup dry white wine
1½ pounds tomatoes, peeled and chopped, or 1 29-once can
    tomatoes, drained
½ teaspoon freshly ground black pepper
⅛ teaspoon nutmeg
¼ cup pine nuts or sliced almonds
2 tablespoons seedless raisins

Have the oxtails cut up. Wash well, place in a saucepan, cover with water and add the carrot, parsley and half the salt. Bring to a boil and cook over medium heat 1½ hours. Drain well. (Reserve liquid for stock, if you like.)

Melt the butter in a saucepan; sauté the onions, celery and ham 5 minutes. Add the oxtails; cook 10 minutes. Mix in the wine; cook until evaporated. Add the tomatoes, pepper, nutmeg and remaining salt. Cover and cook over low heat 1 hour or until the oxtails are tender. Mix in the nuts and raisins; cook 5 minutes longer.

SERVES : 6–8

Pollame

POULTRY

It is only in the north of Italy that chicken is a worthwhile dish. From Naples to Taormina, the local poultry is inclined to be scrawny and somewhat tasteless, if my friends from that region will forgive me for saying so. But in the upper half of the country, from Rome to the Swiss border, chicken is delicious.

A fine bird is often simply roasted over an open fire, after first being seasoned with salt and pepper and rubbed with a few herbs. Around Florence and Bologna, the local chefs prepare some superb poultry dishes, using both chicken and turkey. Incidentally, to the surprise of many Americans, turkey is now a classic holiday dish, just as it is in America. A favorite way of preparing chicken is with a combination of ham and cheese, a cookery style which may be found all across the northern half of Italy. Chicken casseroles, often made with wine, are delicately flavored and constitute a perfect one-meal dish in the American tradition.

Spezzato di Pollo alla Surut

CHICKEN WITH CHICKEN LIVER SAUCE

2 2½-pound chickens, chopped up
2 tablespoons olive oil
4 tablespoons butter
2 teaspoons salt
½ teaspoon freshly ground black pepper
1 clove garlic, minced
2 tablespoons chopped chives or green onions
¾ cup diced mushrooms
1½ cups dry white wine
½ cup chicken broth
½ pound chicken livers, cut in half
2 tablespoons minced parsley

Have the chicken chopped up, bone and all, in small pieces. Wash and dry well. Heat the oil and 2 tablespoons butter in a deep skillet; sauté the chicken in it until browned. Sprinkle with the salt and pepper. Mix in the garlic and chives, then add the mushrooms, wine and broth. Bring to a boil and cook over medium heat 30 minutes or until chicken is tender.

Melt the remaining butter in a separate skillet; sauté the livers in it 5 minutes, or until very little pink remains. Season with a little salt and pepper. Add to the chicken; cook 5 minutes longer. Sprinkle with the parsley.

SERVES : 6–8

Pollo Novello e Peperoni

CHICKEN WITH PEPPERS

5-pound pullet, disjointed
2 teaspoons salt
⅛ teaspoon black pepper
¾ cup minced onions

1 clove garlic, minced
4 tablespoons butter
2 cups chopped tomatoes
3 peppers (green and red), cut in narrow strips
3 tablespoons olive oil
¼ cup grated Romano cheese or Parmesan
2 tablespoons minced parsley

Season the chicken with the salt and pepper. Sauté the onions and garlic in the butter 10 minutes; add the chicken. Cook until browned. Add the tomatoes and broth. Cover and cook over low heat 20 minutes. While the chicken is cooking, sauté the peppers in the olive oil. Add to the chicken and cook 20 minutes longer, or until the chicken is tender. Remove the chicken and stir the cheese and parsley into the gravy. Taste for seasoning; pour over the chicken.

SERVES : 4–6

Pollo ai Castelli Romani

CHICKEN, CASTELLI ROMANI STYLE

3½-pound fryer, disjointed
2 teaspoons salt
½ teaspoon freshly ground black pepper
2 slices bacon, diced
2 tablespoons butter
2 tablespoons olive oil
1 clove garlic, minced
¼ teaspoon rosemary
½ cup dry white wine
2 teaspoons tomato paste
½ cup chicken broth

Wash and dry the chicken pieces; rub with the salt and pepper. In a Dutch oven or heavy frying pan, brown the bacon. Pour off the fat; add the butter and oil and heat. Add the chicken and garlic; sauté until browned. Mix in the rosemary and wine;

cook over low heat 15 minutes. Mix the tomato paste and broth; add to the chicken. Cover and cook over low heat 30 minutes or until chicken is tender.

SERVES : 4

Pollo alla Romana

CHICKEN, ROMAN STYLE

5-pound capon or roasting chicken, disjointed
¼ cup flour
2 teaspoons salt
½ teaspoon freshly ground black pepper
4 tablespoons butter
½ cup finely chopped onions
¼ cup julienne-cut ham
⅓ cup dry white wine
¼ teaspoon rosemary
1½ cups peeled chopped tomatoes

Rub the chicken pieces with a mixture of the flour, salt and pepper. Melt 2 tablespoons butter in a skillet (with oven-proof handle); brown the chicken in it. Remove. Melt the remaining butter in the skillet; sauté the onions and ham 5 minutes. Return the chicken and add the wine and rosemary; cook over low heat until wine is absorbed. Add the tomatoes. Cover and bake in a 350° oven 1 hour or until chicken is tender. Taste for seasoning.

SERVES : 4–5

Variation:

Pollo alla Romana con Peperoni

CHICKEN WITH PEPPERS

Fifteen minutes before chicken is tender, add 2 sliced, sautéed green peppers and 1 clove minced garlic.

Spezzato di Pollo alla Cacciatora

CHICKEN IN RED WINE, HUNTER'S STYLE

5-pound pullet, disjointed
¼ cup olive oil
¾ cup chopped onions
1 green pepper, thinly sliced
1 clove garlic, minced
1½ teaspoons salt
½ teaspoon black pepper
¼ teaspoon oregano
1 cup peeled chopped tomatoes
¾ cup dry red wine
¼ pound mushrooms, sliced

Wash and dry the chicken. Heat the oil in a Dutch oven or deep skillet; brown the chicken in it. Add the onions, green pepper, garlic, salt, pepper and oregano; cook 10 minutes. Mix in the tomatoes and wine; cover and cook over low heat 30 minutes, or until chicken is almost tender. Add the mushrooms; recover and cook 15 minutes longer. Taste for seasoning.

SERVES : 4–6

Casseruola di Pollo

CHICKEN CASSEROLE

3½-pound fryer, disjointed
2 tablespoons flour
2 teaspoons salt
½ teaspoon freshly ground black pepper
¼ cup olive oil
1 clove garlic, minced
½ cup dry white wine
1 cup peeled diced tomatoes
⅛ teaspoon rosemary

2 tablespoons minced parsley
¼ pound mushrooms, sliced
2 tablespoons butter

Rub the chicken with a mixture of the flour, salt and
pepper. Heat the oil in a heavy skillet; brown the chicken in it.
Add the garlic, wine, tomatoes, rosemary and parsley. Cover and
cook over low heat 20 minutes or until the chicken is tender.
Sauté the mushrooms in the butter while the chicken is cooking.
Add to the chicken just before serving.

SERVES : 4

Fricassea di Pollo

CHICKEN FRICASSEE

3½-pound fryer, disjointed
¼ cup olive oil
1 cup chopped onions
½ cup dry white wine
1 clove garlic, minced
2 anchovy fillets
2 tablespoons capers
2 tablespoons pine nuts or sliced almonds
½ cup chopped parsley
2 teaspoons salt
½ teaspoon black pepper
1 teaspoon rosemary

Wash and dry the chicken pieces. Heat the oil in a Dutch
oven or heavy saucepan; brown the chicken in it. Remove the
chicken, and in the fat remaining, brown the onions. Return the
chicken; add the wine and cook until evaporated. Pound together
the garlic, anchovies, capers, nuts, parsley, salt, pepper and rosemary. Mix into the chicken very well to coat the pieces. Cover and
cook over low heat 1 hour or until chicken is tender. Add small

amounts of boiling water from time to time to keep chicken from burning. There should be a thick, but small amount of gravy when chicken is finished.

SERVES : 4

Pollo Piccante

CHICKEN IN SPICY SAUCE

3½-pound fryer, disjointed
3 tablespoons olive oil
3 cloves garlic, sliced
1 teaspoon salt
⅛ teaspoon pepper
½ cup dry white wine
2 tablespoons vinegar
½ cup sliced ripe black olives
¼ cup boiling water
2 anchovy fillets, chopped

Wash and dry the chicken.

Heat the oil in a skillet; add chicken and garlic, sprinkle with salt and pepper and brown over low heat on all sides. Add wine and vinegar; cook 5 minutes. Add olives, water and the chopped anchovies. Cook over low heat 45 minutes or until chicken is tender. Taste for seasoning.

SERVES : 4

Costolette di Pollo

CHICKEN BREASTS WITH CHEESE SAUCE

3 whole raw chicken breasts
1½ teaspoons salt
¼ teaspoon white pepper

3 tablespoons flour
4 tablespoons butter
½ cup milk
3 tablespoons grated Parmesan cheese
2 tablespoons grated Swiss cheese

Cut the chicken breasts in half through the breast bone. Remove the skin and bones. Place between two sheets of waxed paper and pound very thin. Rub with a mixture of the salt, pepper and 2 tablespoons flour.

Melt 3 tablespoons butter in a skillet; brown the chicken in it. Transfer to a shallow baking dish.

Melt 1 tablespoon butter in a saucepan; blend in the remaining flour. Gradually add the milk, stirring steadily to the boiling point; cook over low heat 5 minutes. Mix in the cheeses until melted. Spread over the chicken. Bake in a preheated 375° oven 10 minutes or until browned.

SERVES : 6

Petti di Pollo al Prosciutto

BREAST OF CHICKEN AND HAM

3 whole raw chicken breasts
¼ cup flour
1½ teaspoons salt
¼ teaspoon white pepper
2 tablespoons butter
2 tablespoons olive oil
6 sage leaves or ½ teaspoon dried
6 slices prosciutto ham
½ cup dry white wine

Cut the chicken breasts in half through the breast bone. Remove the skin and bones. Place between 2 sheets of waxed paper and pound very thin. Dip in a mixture of the flour, salt and pepper.

Heat the butter and oil in a skillet; sauté the chicken breasts until browned on the underside. Turn over and place a sage leaf on each or sprinkle with the dried sage. Cover with the ham. Sauté 5 minutes. Add the wine; bring to a boil and cook over low heat 2 minutes. Transfer chicken to a heated serving dish. Scrape the pan and pour the juices over the chicken.

SERVES : 6

Petto di Pollo Mimosa

BREAST OF CHICKEN WITH
CHEESE AND HAM

3 whole raw chicken breasts
2 eggs, beaten
1½ teaspoons salt
¼ teaspoon white pepper
½ cup flour
6 tablespoons butter
6 slices prosciutto or cooked ham
6 slices mozzarella cheese
½ cup chicken broth

Cut the breasts in half through the breast bone. Remove the skin and bones. Place between 2 sheets of waxed paper and pound thin. Dip in a mixture of the eggs, salt and pepper, then in the flour.

Melt the butter in a skillet; brown the chicken on both sides. Place a slice of ham on each chicken piece and cover with a slice of cheese. Add the broth; cover and cook over low heat 5 minutes.

SERVES : 6

Note: Slices of raw turkey breast may be prepared in the same manner.

Pollo alla Diavola

DEVILED BROILED CHICKEN

2 2-pound broilers, split
2 teaspoons salt
½ teaspoon crushed dried red peppers
5 tablespoons olive oil
⅓ cup finely chopped onions
2 tablespoons minced parsley
⅓ cup dry vermouth

Wash and dry the broilers; rub with the salt and red peppers. Brush with the oil. Place in a broiling pan, skin side down. Broil 4 inches from the heat 20 minutes. Turn skin side up and broil 20 minutes longer, spreading with a mixture of the onions and parsley after 10 minutes. Transfer the chickens to a serving dish. Place the broiling pan over direct heat. Add the vermouth; bring to a boil, scraping the pan of all browned particles. Cook 1 minute and pour over the broilers.

SERVES : 4

Pollo Arrostito alla Parmigiana

ROAST CHICKEN WITH CHEESE

3½-pound frying chicken, disjointed
1½ teaspoons salt
½ teaspoon black pepper
2 cloves garlic, minced
4 tablespoons olive oil
½ cup minced onions
4 potatoes, peeled and halved
¾ cup grated Romano or Parmesan cheese
¼ cup chopped parsley
1 cup boiling water

Wash and dry the chicken pieces. Rub with a mixture of the salt, pepper and garlic. Heat the oil in a casserole or Dutch oven; brown the chicken and onions in it. Put the potatoes between the chicken pieces; sprinkle with the cheese and parsley. Bake in a 350° oven 20 minutes. Add the water; cover and bake 30 minutes longer or until chicken and potatoes are tender. Baste a few times.

SERVES : 4

Pollo alla Piemontese

CHICKEN, PIEDMONT STYLE

½ cup olive oil
2 tablespoons lemon juice
¼ cup minced onion
2 tablespoons minced parsley
1½ teaspoons salt
3-pound frying chicken, disjointed
¾ cup sifted flour
½ cup water
1 egg white

Mix together ¼ cup oil, the lemon juice, onion, parsley and half the salt. Rub into the chicken very well and let stand 2 hours. Prepare the batter, meanwhile.

Beat together the flour, water and remaining salt and oil. Let stand 1 hour. Beat the egg white until stiff and fold into the batter. Dip the chicken pieces in it, coating them well. Arrange on a greased baking pan. Bake in a 425° oven 45 minutes, turning the pieces once.

SERVES : 4

Pollo Fiorentina

FRIED MARINATED CHICKEN

3-pound fryer, disjointed
2 tablespoons lemon juice
¼ cup olive oil
1½ teaspoons salt
½ teaspoon freshly ground black pepper
½ cup flour
2 eggs, beaten
1 tablespoon milk
1½ cups olive or vegetable oil

Wash and dry the chicken. Marinate for 4 hours in a mixture of the lemon juice, olive oil, salt and pepper. Baste and turn frequently. Remove the chicken parts and dry with paper towels. Roll in the flour, then dip in the eggs beaten with the milk.

Heat the 1½ cups oil in a skillet until it bubbles. Brown the chicken it in on all sides. Cover loosely and cook over low heat 15 minutes or until tender. Drain on absorbent paper.

SERVES : 4

Spezzatino di Pollo Fritto

GARLIC-FRIED CHICKEN

3½-pound frying chicken
1 egg, beaten
¾ cup flour
2 teaspoons salt
½ teaspoon black pepper
3 cloves garlic, put through a garlic press or mashed to a paste
½ cup vegetable oil
½ cup olive oil
2 whole cloves garlic

Have the butcher chop the chicken, bones and all, into
1-inch pieces. Wash and dry the pieces. Dip in the egg, then in
a mixture of the flour, salt, pepper and mashed garlic. Let stand
a few minutes to dry.

Heat the oils in a skillet; add the whole cloves of garlic. When
browned, remove. Add the chicken pieces. Fry until browned and
tender. Serve garnished with lemon wedges.

SERVES : 4

Piccioni coi Piselli

SQUABS WITH PEAS

4 squabs
1 tablespoon salt
¾ teaspoon freshly ground black pepper
½ teaspoon basil
3 tablespoons butter
1 cup chopped onions
¼ pound ham, julienne-cut
¾ cup dry white wine
¾ cup chicken broth
1 pound green peas, shelled or 1 package frozen, thawed peas

Wash and dry the squabs; rub inside and out with a
mixture of the salt, pepper and basil. Melt the butter in a Dutch
oven or deep heavy skillet; sauté the onions 10 minutes. Add the
squabs; brown on all sides. Mix in the ham and wine; cook over
medium heat 10 minutes. Add the broth; cover and cook over low
heat 30 minutes. Add the peas; recover and cook 15 minutes. Taste
for seasoning. Transfer the squabs to a serving dish and pour
gravy over all.

SERVES : 4

Faraona o Gallo in Salsa di Capperi

GUINEA HEN OR CHICKEN IN
CAPER SAUCE

2-pound guinea hen or broiler, quartered
3 tablespoons butter
1 teaspoon salt
1 tablespoon flour
¾ cup dry white wine
4 anchovy fillets, mashed
2 tablespoons drained capers
2 tablespoons lemon juice

Wash, clean and dry the hen. Melt half the butter in a deep skillet. Brown the hen in it very well. Season with the salt and stir in the flour until browned. Add the wine, anchovies, capers and lemon juice. Stir in remaining butter. Cover and cook over low heat 30 minutes or until tender. Turn the hen quarters once or twice during the cooking time.

SERVES : 2–4

Cappone Arrosto

ROAST CAPON WITH CAPER SAUCE

5-pound capon
1 tablespoon salt
½ teaspoon freshly ground black pepper
3 tablespoons warmed cognac
3 cups chicken broth
2 tablespoons butter
2 tablespoons flour
1 egg yolk
1 cup heavy cream
1 tablespoon chopped capers

Wash and dry the capon; rub with a mixture of the salt and pepper. Place in a shallow buttered roasting pan; roast in a 400° oven 20 minutes. Pour the cognac over it and set aflame; when flames die, add the broth. Reduce heat to 350° and roast 1½ hours longer, or until tender, basting frequently. Pour off the pan juices and reserve.

Melt the butter in a saucepan; blend in the flour. Add the pan juices, stirring constantly to the boiling point; cook over low heat 5 minutes. Beat the egg yolk and cream in a bowl; gradually add the hot sauce, stirring steadily to prevent curdling. Return to saucepan; cook over low heat, stirring steadily, until thickened, but do not let boil. Mix in the capers and taste for seasoning.

Carve the capon and pour sauce over it.

SERVES : 4–5

Crocchette di Pollo con Prosciutto

CHICKEN–HAM CROQUETTES

2 tablespoons butter
2 tablespoons flour
¾ cup light cream
2 tablespoons grated Parmesan cheese
1½ cups chopped cooked chicken
1 cup chopped cooked ham
2 egg yolks, beaten
1 teaspoon salt
¼ teaspoon white pepper
¾ cup fine bread crumbs
Vegetable oil for deep frying

Melt the butter in a saucepan; blend in the flour. Add the cream, stirring steadily to the boiling point; cook over low heat 10 minutes. The sauce should be very thick. Remove from the

heat and stir in the cheese. Cool, then mix in the chicken, ham, egg yolks, salt and pepper. Taste for seasoning and chill 3 hours.

Shape the mixture into 6–8 croquettes. Roll in the bread crumbs. Heat the fat to 370° and fry the croquettes until browned. Drain.

SERVES : 3–4

Anitra all'Olive

DUCK WITH OLIVE SAUCE

5–6 pound duck, disjointed
2 teaspoons salt
½ teaspoon black pepper
½ teaspoon oregano
¾ cup chopped onions
½ cup diced celery
½ cup dry red wine
1 cup beef broth
1 bay leaf
1 cup pitted Italian or Greek olives

Wash the duck, remove as much fat as possible and dry. Rub the pieces with a mixture of the salt, pepper and oregano. In a Dutch oven or heavy casserole, brown the duck pieces on all sides. Pour off the fat. Add the onions and celery; cook 10 minutes. Pour off the fat again. Add the wine, broth, and bay leaf; bring to a boil, cover and cook over low heat 1 hour or until tender. Baste frequently. Arrange the duck on a heated serving dish and keep warm.

Skim the fat off the gravy. Remove bay leaf. Add the olives; cook 5 minutes. Pour some sauce over the duck, and serve the rest in a sauceboat.

SERVES : 4

Anitra in Agrodolce

DUCK IN SWEET-AND-SOUR SAUCE

5–6 pound duck, disjointed
½ cup flour
2 teaspoons salt
½ teaspoon freshly ground black pepper
2 tablespoons butter
1½ cups thinly sliced onions
1½ cups boiling water
½ cup dry white wine
⅛ teaspoon ground cloves
4 tablespoons sugar
3 tablespoons water
3 tablespoons wine vinegar

Remove as much fat as possible from the duck, wash and dry. Roll in a mixture of the flour, salt and pepper.

Melt the butter in a Dutch oven or heavy casserole; brown the duck and onions in it. Pour off the fat. Add the boiling water, wine and cloves; cover and cook over low heat 1½ hours, or until tender. Shake the pan and turn the pieces frequently. Remove the duck; skim the fat from the gravy.

Cook the sugar and 3 tablespoons water until it turns caramel color; stir into the gravy with the vinegar; cook 5 minutes. Taste for seasoning. Serve in a sauceboat.

SERVES : 4

Anitra Arrostita

ROAST STUFFED DUCK

5–6 pound duck
2 teaspoons salt
½ teaspoon black pepper
2 cloves garlic, minced
2 tablespoons olive oil
¾ cup minced onions

1 pound Italian sausages or sausage meat
3 slices toast, diced
⅛ teaspoon crushed dried red peppers
½ teaspoon rosemary
½ cup chopped black olives
½ cup Marsala wine or sweet sherry

Wash and dry the duck; rub inside and out with the salt, pepper and garlic.

Heat the oil in a skillet; sauté the onions 5 minutes. If sausages are used, remove the casings and chop the meat. Add the chopped sausages or sausage meat to the onions; let brown. Pour off the fat. Mix in the diced toast, red peppers, rosemary and olives. Stuff the duck. Close the opening with skewers or sew it. Place in a roasting pan. Roast in a 425° oven 30 minutes. Pour off the fat. Reduce heat to 350°. Roast 30 minutes. Pour off the fat. Add the wine; roast 1½ hours longer, or until tender, basting frequently.

SERVES : 4–5

Anitra alla Casalinga

DUCK CASSEROLE

5–6 pound duck
1 tablespoon butter
4 slices prosciutto or cooked ham, cut julienne
6 small white onions
2 leeks, sliced
1 carrot, sliced
1 clove garlic, minced
2 teaspoons salt
½ teaspoon freshly ground black pepper
1½ cups dry white wine
1 cup chicken broth
2 cups shelled peas
½ pound green beans, cut

½ pound mushrooms, sliced
1½ cups cubed potatoes

Wash the duck parts, remove as much fat as possible and
dry. Melt the butter in a casserole or Dutch oven. Brown the
duck in it on all sides. Pour off the fat. Add the ham, onions,
leeks, carrot, garlic, salt and pepper; cook 5 minutes. Add the
wine and broth. Cover and cook over low heat 45 minutes. Skim
the fat, then add the peas, beans, mushrooms and potatoes. Cook
25 minutes longer. Taste for seasoning.

SERVES : 4

Filetto di Tacchino con Formaggio

TURKEY ROLLS

1 whole raw turkey breast
¼ cup flour
2 teaspoons salt
¼ teaspoon white pepper
6 thin slices prosciutto or cooked ham
6 thin slices mozzarella or Swiss cheese
6 cooked asparagus tips
6 tablespoons butter
½ cup Marsala or sweet sherry
¼ cup chicken broth

Have the turkey breast cut in half through the breast
bone. Remove the skin and bones. Cut each breast half into three
thin fillets. Pound each as thin as possible. Dip the fillets in a
mixture of the flour, salt and pepper. Place a slice of ham on
each, then a slice of cheese and an asparagus. Roll up carefully
and tie with thread or fasten with toothpicks.
Melt 4 tablespoons butter in a skillet; sauté the rolls over very
low heat until tender and browned. Transfer to a heated serving

dish. To the skillet, add the wine, broth and remaining butter. Bring to a boil, scraping the pan of browned particles. Pour over the rolls.

SERVES : 6

Note: Chicken breasts may be prepared in the same manner.

Tacchino Ripieno

STUFFED TURKEY

12-pound turkey
1 tablespoon salt
½ teaspoon freshly ground black pepper
1½ pounds chestnuts
2 tablespoons olive oil
¼ pound ground veal
¼ pound ground beef
1 Italian sausage, chopped
½ cup chopped onions
1 clove garlic, minced
½ cup chopped prunes
½ cup dry white wine
½ cup grated Parmesan cheese
⅛ teaspoon thyme
2 eggs, beaten
4 tablespoons melted butter
1 onion, sliced
1 bay leaf
2 cups water

Wash and dry the turkey. Rub inside and out with the salt and pepper.

Make a criss-cross cut in the pointed end of the chestnuts. Cover with water, bring to a boil and cook over low heat 20 minutes. Drain, cool and remove the shells and inner skin. Chop coarsely.

Heat the oil in a skillet; sauté the veal, beef, sausage, onions and garlic 5 minutes, stirring almost constantly. Remove from the heat; mix in the prunes, wine, cheese, thyme, eggs and chestnuts. Cool, then stuff the turkey. Close the opening with skewers or aluminum foil. Place in a roasting pan and brush with the butter. Add the sliced onion and bay leaf. Roast in a 350° oven 1 hour. Add 1 cup water; roast 1½ hours longer or until tender, basting frequently. Add the remaining water from time to time. Transfer to a heated platter and serve with the strained pan juices.

SERVES : 10–12

Salse

SAUCES

There is a basic difference between sauces in France and Italy. In France, sauces are customarily served separately, but in Italy, they generally form an integral part of the dish itself. Northern Italian sauces are light and delicate, whereas those of southern Italy are, as a rule, heavily spiced, usually made with tomatoes, a great deal of garlic and olive oil, or a combination of those ingredients. In the north, butter and olive oil are frequently combined and sauces are subtle, herbs and spices being used with a degree of delicacy. These sauces are seldom complicated, unlike their French counterparts, and may be readily prepared. Anyone with a home freezer should make up fairly large quantities of them, thus permitting unusual dishes to be prepared swiftly. The north has many superb sauces, most of which will be novel to Americans.

167

Salsa di Pomodoro

TOMATO SAUCE

2 slices bacon, diced
2 tablespoons olive oil
½ cup chopped onions
1 stalk celery, chopped
½ cup grated carrots
4 basil leaves, chopped
2 20-ounce Italian solid pack tomatoes, sieved
1½ teaspoons salt
½ teaspoon freshly ground black pepper

Cook the bacon in the olive oil 2 minutes, then add the onions, celery, carrots and basil. (Try to get fresh basil—if you can't, use ½ teaspoon dried, but add with the salt and pepper.) Sauté 10 minutes, then mix in the tomatoes, salt and pepper. Bring to a boil, cover loosely and cook over low heat 1 hour. Taste for seasoning. Serve with any pasta, or use as directed in recipes.

MAKES : ABOUT 1 QUART

Salsa di Pomodoro "Ammiraglio"

UNCOOKED TOMATO SAUCE

2 pounds ripe tomatoes, peeled
½ pound fresh basil
6 whole cloves garlic
2 teaspoons salt
½ teaspoon freshly ground black pepper
1 cup olive oil

Dice the tomatoes over an earthenware crock or glass bowl, so as to catch all the juice. Wash the basil, dry between paper towels, discard stems and chop fine. Add to the tomatoes with the garlic, salt and pepper. Mix well with a wooden spoon. Pour the olive oil over the top. Cover and chill 1 hour. Discard the garlic, mix well and taste for seasoning. Serve cold with cold meat or shellfish or heat, but do not boil, to serve with a pasta.

MAKES : ABOUT 3½ CUPS

Salsa Genovese

MEAT SAUCE, GENOA STYLE

3 dried mushrooms
3 tablespoons butter
¼ cup chopped onions
¼ cup grated carrots
¼ cup chopped celery
½ cup ground veal
2 tablespoons flour
2 cups peeled chopped tomatoes
1½ teaspoons salt
½ teaspoon freshly ground black pepper
¼ cup dry white wine
1½ cups chicken broth

Wash the mushrooms, cover with warm water and let soak 15 minutes. Drain, and slice fine.

Melt the butter in a saucepan; sauté the onions, carrots and celery 5 minutes. Add the veal and mushrooms; cook over medium heat until browned, stirring almost constantly. Blend in the flour, then the tomatoes; cook 3 minutes. Stir in the salt, pepper, wine and broth. Cover and cook over low heat 45 minutes. Taste for seasoning. Serve with pasta.

MAKES : ABOUT 3 CUPS

Salsa Bolognese

BOLOGNESE SAUCE

2 tablespoons butter
¼ cup diced ham
½ cup chopped onions
¼ cup grated carrots
¼ cup chopped celery
¾ pound ground beef
¼ pound ground pork
½ cup dry white wine
2 tablespoons tomato paste
3 cups beef broth
½ teaspoon salt
½ teaspoon freshly ground black pepper
⅛ teaspoon nutmeg
¼ pound mushrooms, sliced
½ cup heavy cream (optional)

Melt the butter in a saucepan; lightly brown the ham. Add the onions, carrots and celery; cook over low heat 5 minutes. Add the beef and pork; cook, stirring almost steadily for 5 minutes. Mix in the wine; cook until evaporated. Stir in the tomato paste, 1 cup broth, the salt, pepper and nutmeg. Cook over low heat 15 minutes. Add the mushrooms and remaining broth; cover and cook over low heat 45 minutes. Taste for seasoning. Mix in the cream if you like. The sauce can be served either way. Serve with any pasta.

MAKES : ABOUT 4½ CUPS

Salsa di Carne

MEAT SAUCE

1 pound ground beef
2 tablespoons flour

4 tablespoons olive oil
¾ cup chopped onions
¼ cup grated carrots
1 tablespoon minced parsley
¾ cup dry red wine
1 20-ounce can Italian-style tomatoes
1½ cups beef broth
¾ cup chopped mushrooms
1½ teaspoons salt
½ teaspoon freshly ground black pepper

Toss the beef with the flour. Heat the oil in a saucepan; sauté the onions, carrots and parsley 10 minutes. Add the beef; cook until no red remains, stirring frequently to prevent lumps from forming. Add the wine; cook over high heat 3 minutes. Mix in the tomatoes, broth, mushrooms, salt and pepper. Cook over low heat 1½ hours. Taste for seasoning. Serve with any pasta.

MAKES : ABOUT 3 CUPS

Salsa di Polpette

MEAT-BALL SAUCE

2 slices white bread
1 cup water
½ pound ground beef
½ pound ground pork
½ cup grated Parmesan cheese
2½ teaspoons salt
1 teaspoon black pepper
½ teaspoon basil
2 cloves garlic, minced
2 tablespoons olive oil
½ cup chopped onions
1 29-ounce can Italian-style tomatoes
1 cup water
¼ teaspoon crushed dried red peppers

Soak the bread in the water. Mash smooth and press dry. Mix together the bread, beef, pork, cheese, 1 teaspoon salt, the pepper, basil and 1 clove garlic. Shape into walnut-sized balls.

Heat the oil in a skillet; brown the meat balls in it. Add the onions, tomatoes, water, red peppers, remaining salt and garlic. Bring to a boil and cook over low heat 1½ hours. Taste for seasoning. Serve on spaghetti or use as directed in recipes.

MAKES : ABOUT 5 CUPS

Salsa di Fegatini

CHICKEN LIVER SAUCE

5 dried mushrooms
1 pound chicken livers
3 tablespoons flour
4 tablespoons butter
1 teaspoon salt
¼ teaspoon freshly ground black pepper
⅓ cup Marsala or sweet sherry
1½ cups chicken broth
2 tablespoons minced parsley

Wash the mushrooms, cover with warm water and let soak 15 minutes. Drain and chop.

Wash the livers, remove any discolored areas and dry. Dice the livers and toss with the flour.

Melt the butter in a saucepan; sauté the livers and mushrooms 5 minutes. Season with the salt and pepper and add the wine; cook over medium heat 3 minutes. Add the broth; cook over low heat 20 minutes. Mix in the parsley and taste for seasoning. Serve with pasta, but particularly good with *gnocchi*.

MAKES : ABOUT 2½ CUPS

Salsa con Capperi

CAPER BUTTER SAUCE

¼ pound sweet butter
⅛ cup capers
2 teaspoons lemon juice
½ teaspoon salt

Melt the butter and add the capers, lemon juice and salt. Serve with vegetables or fish.

MAKES : ABOUT ¾ CUP

Salsa con Capperi all'Olio

CAPER OIL SAUCE

½ cup olive oil
3 tablespoons lemon juice
½ cup drained capers

Beat the oil and lemon juice together. Stir in the capers. Serve with fish, boiled beef or chicken or with an appetizer salad.

MAKES : ABOUT ¾ CUP

Salsa Besciamella

WHITE SAUCE

2 tablespoons butter
3 tablespoons flour
2 cups hot milk or 2 cups hot chicken broth or 2 cups hot
  fish stock
Salt
White pepper

Melt the butter in a saucepan over low heat. Blend in the flour with a wooden spoon, but do not let it turn color. Remove from the heat and when mixture stops bubbling, beat in the liquid with a wire whisk until smooth. Return to the heat and cook, stirring steadily until it boils. Cook 2 minutes longer, and season to taste with salt and pepper. Use the milk in a sauce intended for vegetables, eggs, cheese, etc.; chicken broth for chicken or veal dishes; and fish stock for fish or seafood.

MAKES : ABOUT 2 CUPS

Salsa Agrodolce, Siciliana

SWEET-AND-SOUR SAUCE

¼ cup olive oil
½ cup chopped onions
¼ cup minced parsley
2 cups peeled diced tomatoes
¾ teaspoon salt
⅛ teaspoon black pepper
¼ teaspoon basil
1 tablespoon sugar
1 teaspoon cinnamon
3 tablespoons wine vinegar

Heat the oil in a saucepan; sauté the onions 5 minutes. Add the parsley; sauté 2 minutes. Mix in the tomatoes, salt, pepper and basil. Cook over low heat 15 minutes. Mix in the sugar, cinnamon and vinegar. Cook 10 minutes longer. Serve with fish or boiled meat.

MAKES : ABOUT 1½ CUPS

Salsa Piccante

PIQUANT SAUCE

3 tablespoons olive oil
1 tablespoon wine vinegar
1 8-ounce can tomato sauce
¾ teaspoon salt
¼ teaspoon black pepper
½ teaspoon sugar
¾ teaspoon dry mustard
4 hard-cooked egg yolks, mashed

In a saucepan, mix together the oil, vinegar, tomato sauce, salt, pepper and sugar. Bring to a boil and cook over low heat 10 minutes, stirring frequently. Remove from the heat and mix in the mustard and egg yolks. Chill. Serve with fish or boiled meat.

MAKES : ABOUT 1¼ CUPS

Salsa di Zabaione

MARSALA CUSTARD SAUCE

3 egg yolks
½ cup sugar
¾ cup Marsala or sweet sherry
1 tablespoon cognac

Beat the egg yolks and sugar together in the top of a double boiler until thick and light. Add the wine and place over hot water. Cook, stirring constantly until thickened. Stir in cognac. Serve hot or cold on fritters, cakes or puddings.

MAKES : 1½ CUPS

Legumi e Insalate

VEGETABLES AND SALADS

In Italy, fresh vegetables come into season and then disappear from the market. When artichokes, for example, are in season every home and restaurant serves artichokes day after day. In the United States, favored by geography with a long season, and aided by canned and frozen products, the distinctive season for each vegetable is somewhat lost.

Italians love fine vegetables and salad greens. They are willing to spend the necessary time to pick perfect specimens of fresh vegetables, with special preference for the very smallest. Large vegetables, they believe, are likely to be overgrown, with a somewhat woody texture. A bruised vegetable, it is true, cannot possibly have the flavor and quality of a perfect specimen. For this reason, although I do not like to rise early in the morning, I force myself to visit the downtown New York produce market at 5 A.M. in order to select personally the vegetables and salad greens for my restaurant. For best results, you too, must per-

176

sonally select vegetables, rejecting all bruised, overage or overgrown specimens.

Simple, boiled vegetables may be served with a main course. Many Italian preparations may (and often should) be served as a separate course, so that your guests will fully appreciate the flavor of the herbs, spices or sauces in your vegetable dishes.

Wine does not go well with vinegar. Thus, in Italy, it is customary to serve salads after the main course, so that the salad dressing will not interfere with the wine. For best results, tear salad greens with the hands, rather than cut them with a knife.

Carciofi alla Diavola

DEVILED ARTICHOKES, ROMAN STYLE

8 small young artichokes
½ cup olive oil
½ cup water
¾ cup chopped parsley
3 cloves garlic, minced
1½ teaspoons salt

Remove the stems of the artichokes, and with a scissors, trim the pointed ends of the leaves. Wash carefully. Arrange the artichokes in an upright position in a shallow casserole or deep skillet. Add the oil and water—the liquid should reach halfway up—if not, add more oil and water. Press a mixture of the parsley and garlic between the leaves of the artichokes and sprinkle with salt. Cover and cook over medium heat 45 minutes. Remove the cover and cook over high heat until artichokes are dry.

SERVES : 8

Carciofi al Burro e Formaggio

ARTICHOKES WITH BUTTER AND CHEESE

1 package frozen artichoke hearts
2 tablespoons olive oil
3 tablespoons butter
½ cup grated Parmesan cheese

Cook the artichokes 2 minutes less than package directs. Drain thoroughly. Put the oil and 1 tablespoon butter in a shallow baking dish. Arrange the artichokes in it in a single layer. Dot with the remaining butter. Bake in a 350° oven 5 minutes. Sprinkle with the cheese, raise heat to 450° and bake 10 minutes longer. Serve directly from the dish.

SERVES : 4

Carciofi alla Romana

ROMAN-STYLE ARTICHOKES

6 small artichokes
2 cloves garlic, minced
1 cup minced parsley
1 teaspoon chopped fresh mint or ⅛ teaspoon dried mint
2 teaspoons salt
½ teaspoon freshly ground black pepper
¼ cup olive oil
1 cup dry white wine
½ cup chicken broth

Buy very young artichokes. Remove the tough outer leaves and cut off the points of the others. Carefully force the centers apart and cut out the chokes. Stuff the centers with a mixture of the garlic, parsley, mint, 1 teaspoon salt and ¼ teaspoon pepper. Arrange close together in a casserole; sprinkle with the oil. Cook over medium heat 10 minutes. Add the wine, broth and remaining salt and pepper. Cover and cook over medium heat 45 minutes or until artichokes are tender.

SERVES : 6

Asparagi alla Parmigiana

ASPARAGUS WITH PARMESAN CHEESE

2 pounds fresh asparagus or 3 packages frozen asparagus tips
½ cup melted butter
½ cup grated Parmesan cheese

Cut the tough ends off the fresh asparagus. Wash carefully and cook until tender but still firm, or cook the frozen asparagus 2 minutes less than package directs. Drain well. Arrange in a single layer in a buttered shallow baking dish. Pour the melted butter over them and sprinkle with the cheese. Bake in a preheated 400° oven 10 minutes or until lightly browned.

SERVES : 6–8

Fagiolini al Pomodoro

GREEN BEANS IN TOMATO SAUCE

¾ cup olive oil
1½ cups thinly sliced onions
2 cups chopped fresh or canned tomatoes
1½ teaspoons salt
½ teaspoon freshly ground black pepper
¼ teaspoon oregano
1½ pounds green beans, cut or 2 packages frozen,
    thawed green beans

Heat the oil in a saucepan; sauté the onions 5 minutes. Mix in the tomatoes, salt, pepper, oregano and beans. Bring to a boil, cover and cook over low heat 1 hour, removing the cover for the last 10 minutes. Serve hot or cold.

SERVES : 4–6

Fagiolini al Prosciutto

GREEN BEANS WITH HAM

2 pounds green beans or 2 packages frozen green beans
4 tablespoons butter
¼ pound prosciutto or cooked ham, cut julienne
¼ teaspoon freshly ground black pepper
2 tablespoons minced parsley
⅛ teaspoon minced garlic

Cook the beans in boiling salted water until tender but firm. Drain.

Melt the butter in a skillet; sauté the ham 3 minutes. Mix in the beans, pepper and salt to taste. Sauté 2 minutes, mixing lightly constantly. Stir in the parsley and garlic.

SERVES : 6–8

Fave Fresche Stufate

LIMA BEANS WITH HAM

3 tablespoons butter
½ cup finely chopped onions
½ cup julienne-cut prosciutto or cooked ham
1 cup shredded lettuce
2 packages frozen lima beans, thawed
1 teaspoon salt

¼ teaspoon freshly ground black pepper
¾ cup boiling water

Melt the butter in a skillet; sauté the onions 5 minutes. Mix in the ham for 1 minute. Add the lettuce, beans, salt, pepper and water. Bring to a boil, cover, and cook over low heat 10 minutes or until tender and liquid absorbed.

SERVES : 6–8

Cavolo Verza all'Acciuga con Salsicce

CABBAGE WITH ANCHOVIES AND SAUSAGES

3 pounds cabbage
2 tablespoons olive oil
2 tablespoons butter
4 anchovy fillets, mashed
¼ cup chopped parsley
½ pound Italian sausages, sliced

Wash the cabbage and cut head in eighths. Cook in boiling salted water 5 minutes. Drain thoroughly.

Heat the oil and butter in a saucepan. Mix in the anchovies and parsley; sauté 3 minutes. Add the cabbage; cover and cook 30 minutes. Lightly brown the sausages; drain and add to the cabbage. Recover and cook 20 minutes longer.

SERVES : 4–6

Carote Agrodolce

SWEET-AND-SOUR CARROTS

10 carrots
1½ cups water

1¼ teaspoons salt
3 tablespoons butter
2 teaspoons flour
2 tablespoons sugar
3 tablespoons cider vinegar

Wash, scrape and slice carrots very thin. Bring the water and salt to a boil in a skillet; add the carrots, cover and cook over low heat 5 minutes. Drain, reserving the liquid.

Melt the butter in a saucepan; blend in the flour, then gradually the liquid, stirring steadily to the boiling point. Mix in the sugar and vinegar, then the carrots. Cook over low heat 5 minutes. Taste for seasoning.

SERVES : 4–6

Cavolfiore Indorato

GOLDEN-FRIED CAULIFLOWER

1 medium head cauliflower or 2 packages frozen cauliflower
¾ cup flour
1 teaspoon salt
¼ teaspoon white pepper
2 eggs, beaten
Vegetable oil for deep frying

Separate fresh cauliflower into flowerets and cook in boiling, salted water until tender but firm. Cook the frozen cauliflower 1 minute less than package directs. Drain well, cool and dry with paper towels. Roll the cauliflower in a mixture of the flour, salt and pepper, then dip in the eggs. Heat the oil to 385°. Fry the cauliflower until browned. Drain.

SERVES : 4–6

Cavolfiore alla Milanese

CAULIFLOWER WITH CHEESE

1 medium-sized cauliflower or 2 packages frozen cauliflower
½ cup grated mozzarella cheese
2 tablespoons grated Parmesan cheese
¼ cup melted butter
2 tablespoons dry bread crumbs

Remove the leaves of the fresh cauliflower and wash thoroughly. Cook in boiling salted water 15 minutes or until tender but firm. Drain. Cook the frozen cauliflower 2 minutes less than package directs. Drain.

Place the cauliflower in a greased baking dish. Mix together the mozzarella cheese, Parmesan cheese, butter, and bread crumbs; spread over the cauliflower. Bake in a 425° oven 5 minutes or until browned.

SERVES : 4–6

Sedani alla Parmigiana

CELERY WITH CHEESE

3 bunches celery
3 tablespoons butter
½ cup beef broth
1 teaspoon salt
¼ teaspoon freshly ground black pepper
¼ cup chopped ham
¼ cup grated Swiss cheese
¼ cup grated Parmesan cheese

Wash the celery and discard the leaves. Cut each bunch in eighths, lengthwise. Melt the butter in a skillet; sauté the celery

5 minutes, shaking the pan frequently. Add the broth, salt, pepper and ham. Cover and cook over low heat 15 minutes, shaking the pan frequently. Drain if any liquid remains. Turn into a buttered baking dish; sprinkle with the mixed cheeses. Bake in a 425° oven 10 minutes or until browned.

SERVES : 6–8

Melanzane alla Parmigiana

BAKED EGGPLANT AND CHEESE

1 medium eggplant
3 teaspoons salt
½ cup flour
¼ cup olive oil
1½ pounds tomatoes, peeled and sliced
½ teaspoon freshly ground black pepper
½ pound mozzarella cheese, thinly sliced
½ cup grated Parmesan cheese
2 tablespoons butter

Peel the eggplant and slice ½-inch thick. Sprinkle with 2 teaspoons salt; let stand 1 hour. Drain and dry thoroughly. Dip in the flour.

Heat 2 tablespoons oil in a skillet; brown the eggplant in it. Put half the slices in a greased baking dish. Cover with half the tomatoes, sprinkled with pepper and remaining salt, slices of cheese and grated cheese. Repeat the sequence of layers. Dot with butter and sprinkle with the remaining oil. Bake in a 350° oven 25 minutes.

SERVES : 4–6

Melanzane-Zucchini Gratinate

EGGPLANT-ZUCCHINI MELANGE

1 medium eggplant
3 teaspoons salt
⅛ cup olive oil
2 cups thinly sliced zucchini
¼ cup finely chopped onions
2 cloves garlic, minced
4 tablespoons dry bread crumbs
2 tablespoons minced parsley
¼ pound mushrooms, sliced and sautéed

Peel the eggplant and cut in 1-inch cubes. Sprinkle with
1½ teaspoons salt and let stand 30 minutes. Drain well and dry.
Heat 2 tablespoons oil in a skillet; brown the eggplant cubes on
all sides. Remove and keep warm.

Heat 2 tablespoons oil in the skillet; sauté the zucchini 10
minutes or until tender. Season with 1 teaspoon salt. Add to the
eggplant.

Heat the remaining oil in the skillet; sauté the onions 3 minutes. Mix in the garlic, bread crumbs, parsley and remaining salt.
Cook over low heat 2 minutes, stirring constantly. Mix in the
mushrooms, then spread over the eggplant and zucchini.

SERVES : 6–8

Parmigiana di Melanzane Con Carne

EGGPLANT-MEAT CASSEROLE

1 medium-sized eggplant
3 tablespoons olive oil
2 teaspoons salt
½ teaspoon freshly ground black pepper
1 pound ground beef
¼ pound calf or chicken livers, diced

2 hard-cooked eggs, diced
¼ cup grated Parmesan cheese
¼ pound mozzarella cheese, thinly sliced
2 tablespoons butter

Peel the eggplant and slice thin. Heat the oil until it bubbles; brown the eggplant slices in it on both sides. Season with 1 teaspoon salt and ¼ teaspoon pepper.

In the same skillet, sauté the meat and liver 5 minutes, stirring almost constantly. Mix in the eggs, 1 tablespoon Parmesan cheese and the remaining salt and pepper.

In a greased casserole, arrange successive layers of the eggplant, meat mixture and mozzarella, starting and ending with the eggplant. Sprinkle with the remaining Parmesan cheese and dot with the butter. Bake in a 350° oven 30 minutes. Serve directly from the casserole.

SERVES : 4–6

Finocchi Dorati

BATTER-FRIED FENNEL

6 fennel
1 egg
3 tablespoons flour
½ cup milk
¾ teaspoon salt
1 cup vegetable oil

Remove the leaves of the fennel, wash carefully and cook in boiling salted water 10 minutes. Drain, cool and cut each head in quarters. Make a batter of the egg, flour, milk and salt. Dip the fennel in it.

Heat the oil in a skillet until it bubbles; fry the fennel in it until browned on all sides. Drain well.

SERVES : 6–8

Funghi Trifolati all'Oregano

SAUTÉED MUSHROOMS WITH OREGANO

1½ pounds mushrooms
4 tablespoons olive oil
3 cloves garlic, minced
¾ teaspoon salt
¼ teaspoon freshly ground black pepper
¼ teaspoon oregano

Wash and dry the mushrooms. Heat the oil in a skillet; mix in the mushrooms, garlic, salt, pepper and oregano. Cook over low heat 10 minutes, stirring frequently.

SERVES : 4

Piselli alla Fiorentina

PEAS, FLORENCE STYLE

¼ cup olive oil
1 pound peas, shelled or 1 package frozen, thawed peas
1 clove garlic
½ cup diced ham
½ cup water
2 tablespoons minced parsley
1 teaspoon salt
¼ teaspoon white pepper

Combine all the ingredients in a saucepan. Bring to a boil and cook over low heat 15 minutes. Taste for seasoning.

SERVES : 3–4

Peperoni alla Romana

GREEN PEPPERS, ROMAN STYLE

4 tablespoons olive oil
2 cups coarsely chopped onions
4 cups coarsely chopped green peppers
1 cup dry white wine
1½ teaspoons salt
¼ teaspoon freshly ground black pepper
2 tablespoons minced parsley

Heat the oil in a skillet; sauté the onions 10 minutes. Add the peppers, wine, salt and pepper. Cook over low heat 25 minutes or until peppers are tender. Sprinkle with the parsley.

SERVES : 4–6

Patate al Forno

BAKED POTATO–TOMATO CASSEROLE

4 potatoes (1½ pounds)
1 tablespoon olive oil
1½ cups sliced onions
2 tomatoes, cut in sixths
1½ teaspoons salt
½ teaspoon freshly ground black pepper
3 tablespoons butter

Peel the potatoes and cut into eighths. Grease a casserole with the oil. Put the potatoes, onions, tomatoes, salt and pepper in it. Dot with the butter. Bake in a 400° oven 50 minutes, or until browned. Mix occasionally.

SERVES : 4–6

Crocchette di Patate

POTATO–CHEESE CROQUETTES

2 pounds potatoes
4 tablespoons butter
3 eggs
1 egg yolk
½ cup grated Parmesan cheese
1¼ teaspoons salt
½ teaspoon white pepper
¼ teaspoon nutmeg
½ cup dry bread crumbs
2 cups vegetable oil

Cook the unpeeled potatoes until tender. Drain, peel and mash very smooth or put through a ricer. Beat in the butter, 1 egg, the egg yolk, cheese, salt, pepper and nutmeg. Chill.

Form into ten to twelve croquettes. Beat the remaining eggs. Dip the croquettes in them, then in the bread crumbs. Heat the oil in a skillet until it bubbles. Fry the croquettes until browned.

SERVES : 6–8

Spinaci con Uvette

SPINACH WITH RAISINS

½ cup seedless raisins
1½ pounds spinach or 2 packages frozen spinach
½ teaspoon salt
1 tablespoon olive oil
2 tablespoons butter
2 tablespoons pine nuts or sliced almonds

Soak the raisins in warm water 15 minutes. Drain well. Wash the fresh spinach, then cook for 5 minutes. Drain well, and season with the salt. Or cook the frozen spinach 1 minute less than package directs. Drain well.

Heat the oil and butter in a skillet; mix in the spinach, raisins and nuts. Cook over low heat 5 minutes, stirring frequently.

SERVES : 4

Spinaci alla Parmigiana

SPINACH WITH CHEESE, PARMA STYLE

2 pounds spinach or 3 packages frozen spinach
1 teaspoon salt
4 tablespoons butter
¾ cup grated Parmesan cheese

Wash the fresh spinach, discard the stems. Combine in a saucepan with the salt, cover and cook over low heat for 5 minutes (do not add any water). Drain thoroughly. Or cook the frozen spinach 1 minute less than package directs. Drain thoroughly.

Melt the butter in a skillet; add the spinach. Cook over low heat 5 minutes, stirring frequently. Mix in the cheese. Taste for seasoning.

SERVES : 4-6

Pomodori Gratinati

BAKED TOMATOES

4 large firm tomatoes
¾ cup dry bread crumbs
3 tablespoons finely chopped parsley
1 clove garlic, minced

1¼ teaspoons salt
¼ teaspoon freshly ground black pepper
¼ cup olive oil

Buy even-sized tomatoes. Cut in half crosswise. Mix together the bread crumbs, parsley, garlic, salt, pepper and 2 tablespoons oil. Spread on the cut side of the tomatoes. Arrange in an oiled shallow baking pan; sprinkle with the remaining oil. Bake in a 400° oven 15 minutes or until tomatoes are tender.

SERVES : 4–8

Pomodori Ripieni

RICE-STUFFED TOMATOES

6 large firm tomatoes
¼ cup olive oil
½ cup chopped onions
½ cup raw rice
½ cup boiling water
2 teaspoons salt
¼ teaspoon freshly ground black pepper
¼ teaspoon basil
¼ cup grated mozzarella cheese

Buy even-sized tomatoes. Cut a 1-inch piece off the stem end of the tomatoes. Scoop out the pulp and reserve.

Heat 2 tablespoons oil in a skillet; sauté the onions 5 minutes. Mix in the rice until translucent. Add the tomato pulp, water, salt, pepper and basil. Cook over low heat 10 minutes. Cool and stir in the cheese. Stuff the tomatoes; arrange in an oiled baking dish; sprinkle with the remaining oil. Cover and bake in a 350° oven 45 minutes, removing the cover for the last 10 minutes. Serve hot or cold.

SERVES : 6

Zucchini Genovese

SAUTÉED ZUCCHINI

1½ pounds small zucchini
4 tablespoons olive oil
1 teaspoon salt
¼ teaspoon freshly ground black pepper
2 tablespoons minced parsley
1 clove garlic, minced
¼ teaspoon oregano

Wash, scrub, and cut off the stem ends of the zucchini. Cut in pencil thin, 3-inch lengths.

Heat the oil in a skillet; cook the zucchini over high heat until browned, shaking the pan frequently. Add the salt, pepper, parsley, garlic, and oregano. Cook over low heat 5 minutes.

SERVES : 4–6

Zucchini in Salsa Verde

ZUCCHINI IN GREEN SAUCE

1½ pounds small zucchini
⅓ cup flour
1½ teaspoons salt
Vegetable oil for deep frying
⅓ cup olive oil
¼ cup minced parsley
3 tablespoons wine vinegar
2 anchovies, minced
1 clove garlic, minced
½ teaspoon freshly ground black pepper

Wash, scrub and thinly slice the zucchini. Toss in a mixture of the flour and salt. Heat the vegetable oil to 380°. Fry the zucchini until browned. Drain well.

Mix together the olive oil, parsley, vinegar, anchovies, garlic, and pepper. Pour over the zucchini and let marinate 2 hours, turning the mixture occasionally. Serve at room temperature.

SERVES : 4–6

Zucchini Ripiene

STUFFED ZUCCHINI

3 medium zucchini
⅓ cup olive oil
½ cup minced onions
1 pound ground beef
2 teaspoons salt
½ teaspoon freshly ground pepper
¼ teaspoon oregano
½ cup canned tomato sauce

Buy straight, plump zucchini. Wash, dry, and remove the stems. Cut in half lengthwise. Scoop out the pulp and chop it. Reserve the shells.

Heat 2 tablespoons oil in a skillet; sauté the onions 5 minutes. Mix in the zucchini pulp; sauté 5 minutes. Add the beef; cook until no pink remains, stirring frequently to prevent lumps from forming. Mix in the salt, pepper, and oregano. Stuff the shells. Arrange in an oiled baking dish. Sprinkle with the remaining oil and cover with tomato sauce. Bake in a 350° oven 40 minutes. Taste sauce for seasoning.

SERVES : 6

Insalata di Cicoria

CHICORY SALAD

2 heads chicory
2 cloves garlic, minced
¼ cup minced onions
⅓ cup olive oil
2 tablespoons wine vinegar
1 teaspoon salt
½ teaspoon black pepper

Wash the chicory very well. Discard tough outer leaves.
Dry well. Tear (don't cut) the leaves into a bowl. Toss with the
garlic and onions. Mix together the oil, vinegar, salt and pepper.
Pour over the chicory. Toss.

SERVES : 6–8

Insalata di Pomodori Ripieni

STUFFED TOMATO SALAD

6 firm tomatoes
1 can anchovy fillets
¼ cup chopped capers
1 clove garlic, minced
1 tablespoon olive oil
2 hard-cooked eggs, chopped
¼ teaspoon black pepper
1 teaspoon lemon juice

Buy large, even-sized tomatoes. Cut a ½-inch piece from
the stem end. Scoop out the pulp and chop it. Chop the undrained
anchovies; mix with the chopped tomatoes, capers, garlic, olive
oil, eggs, pepper and lemon juice. Stuff the tomatoes. Serve as an
appetizer.

SERVES : 6

Insalata di Aranci

ORANGE SALAD

4 oranges
1 teaspoon black pepper
¼ cup olive oil

Peel the oranges and slice very thin. Sprinkle with the pepper and olive oil. Let stand 30 minutes before serving.

SERVES : 4–6

Note: This salad is particularly good with roast meats and duck.

Insalata Primavera

SPRING SALAD

⅓ cup olive oil
¾ teaspoon salt
½ teaspoon black pepper
1 clove garlic, minced
2 tablespoons wine vinegar
1 head romaine lettuce, shredded
1 cucumber, peeled and sliced
8 radishes, sliced
1 cup julienne-cut green peppers
2 tomatoes, cut in eighths

Mix together the oil, salt, pepper, garlic and wine vinegar. In a bowl, combine the lettuce, cucumber, radishes, green peppers and tomatoes. Pour the dressing over the vegetables, mix well and let stand 5 minutes before serving.

SERVES : 4–6

Insalata Verde

GREEN SALAD

Use crisp green: rocket (an Italian green), escarole, curly endive, thinly-sliced fennel, romaine lettuce or any green. Have them washed and thoroughly dried. The dressing consists of 3 parts olive oil, 1 part wine vinegar, salt, freshly ground black pepper and a little minced garlic, if you like. Toss the dressing with the greens seconds before serving.

Insalata di Cipolla

ONION SALAD

4 large red Italian or sweet Spanish onions
2 teaspoons salt
½ cup olive oil
3 tablespoons wine vinegar
8 anchovy fillets
¼ cup pitted black olives (Italian or Greek)

Peel the onions and slice paper thin. Cover with ice water; add the salt and a few ice cubes. Let stand 30 minutes. Drain and dry the onions. Put the onions in a salad bowl; sprinkle with a mixture of the oil and vinegar. Arrange the anchovies and olives on top.

SERVES : 6–8

Insalata Rinforzata

CAULIFLOWER SALAD

1 head cauliflower or 2 packages frozen cauliflower
2 cans anchovy fillets, drained

1 cup black olives (Italian, if available)
1 tablespoon capers
¼ cup olive oil
2 tablespoons lemon juice
¼ teaspoon freshly ground black pepper

Cook the fresh cauliflower until tender but firm. Drain and separate into flowerets. Or cook the frozen cauliflower flowerets 1 minute less than package directs. Cool.

In a salad bowl, toss together lightly the cauliflower, anchovies, olives and capers. Mix the oil, lemon juice and pepper; pour over the ingredients in the bowl.

SERVES : 4–6

Insalata di Riso

RICE AND VEGETABLE SALAD

1 cup rice
1½ cups boiling water
2 teaspoons salt
1 cup julienne-cut celery root
1 cup sliced bottled artichoke hearts in oil
1 cup sliced sautéed mushrooms
1 7¾-ounce can tuna fish, drained and flaked
1 cup peeled diced tomatoes
½ cup sliced black olives
¼ cup chopped anchovies
¼ cup olive oil
½ teaspoon freshly ground black pepper
½ teaspoon capers
1 red onion, thinly sliced

Cook the rice in the boiling water and 1 teaspoon salt in a covered saucepan 15 minutes or until tender but firm and dry.

Cool and toss with a fork to keep grains separate. Add the celery root, artichokes, mushrooms, tuna fish, tomatoes, olives and anchovies. Toss together with 2 forks, then toss with the oil, pepper, capers and remaining salt. Heap on a serving dish and arrange onion slices on top.

SERVES : 4–6

Insalata di Pasqua

EASTER SALAD

1 pound peas or 1 package frozen peas, cooked, drained and
  cooled
1 can anchovy fillets
¼ pound prosciutto or cooked ham
1 head lettuce, cut in wedges
½ cup olive oil
2 hard-cooked egg yolks, mashed
¼ cup lemon juice
1 teaspoon salt
¼ teaspoon freshly ground black pepper
Black and green olives

Put the peas on the bottom of a salad bowl. Arrange the anchovies and ham over them, then the lettuce wedges around the edge of the bowl. Beat together the oil, egg yolks, lemon juice, salt and pepper. Pour over the ingredients in the bowl. Garnish with olives.

SERVES : 4–6

Insalata al Formaggio

CHEESE SALAD

6 endive
¼ pound Bel Paese cheese, diced
⅓ cup olive oil
2 tablespoons lemon juice
½ teaspoon salt
¼ teaspoon freshly ground black pepper

Wash the endive, dry and cut crosswise in 1-inch pieces. Combine the endive and cheese in salad bowl. Pour over it a mixture of the oil, lemon juice, salt and pepper. Toss lightly.

SERVES : 4–6

I Dolci

DESSERTS

As most Americans know, the Italians usually end their meals with fruit or cheese. Rich cakes, pies or fancy ice-cream desserts, so popular in the United States at the end of a meal, are reserved in Italy for between-meal snacks, receptions or special occasions. Ice-cream desserts are popular on hot summer days in Italy during the late afternoon, or possibly after the theatre. However, most of the recipes in this section would be suitable as a dessert at the conclusion of a dinner.

Certain flavors are particularly appealing to the Italian palate. There is a decided preference for certain nuts, notably almonds and chestnuts, and many desserts are made with these delicious flavoring ingredients. It should be remembered that during the Middle Ages, all cooking innovations originated in northern Italy, which then set the culinary pace for the entire civilized world. This is particularly true with respect to desserts, for it was the Venetian crusaders who first brought sugar to Europe during the twelfth century. It is from this date that the modern art of making *I Dolci,* or sweets, first began.

Zabaione

MARSALA CUSTARD

8 egg yolks
½ cup fine granulated sugar
1 cup Marsala or sweet sherry

In the top of a double boiler, beat the egg yolks and sugar with a wire whisk until thick. Beat in the wine; place over hot water and beat until hot and very thick, but do not let boil. Spoon into tall glasses or sherbet cups and serve immediately.

SERVES : 6–8

Gelato di Mandorla

ALMOND CREAM MOLD

2 eggs
1 tablespoon corn starch
3 cups light cream
½ cup sugar
⅛ teaspoon salt
2 teaspoons almond extract
½ cup blanched chopped almonds

Beat the eggs in the top of a double boiler. Mix in the corn starch, then the cream, sugar, and salt. Place over hot water and cook, stirring constantly until thickened, but do not let boil. Stir in the almond extract; strain. Cool, then mix in the almonds. Turn into a buttered melon mold. Place a piece of buttered waxed paper over the top, then cover mold. Place in freezer section of the refrigerator or home freezer. Freeze 4 hours or until firm. To unmold, hold a hot towel around the mold, then turn out onto a chilled serving dish.

SERVES : 6–8

Monte Bianco

CHESTNUT DESSERT

1½ pounds chestnuts
3 cups milk
1 cup powdered sugar
1 cup heavy cream
2 tablespoons cognac

Cut a crisscross on the pointed end of the chestnuts. Cover with water, bring to a boil and cook over medium heat 15 minutes. Drain, peel and remove the inner skin.

Combine the chestnuts and milk; cook over low heat 45 minutes or until very soft. Drain, mash smooth and beat in the sugar.

Force the chestnut mixture through a ricer or food mill onto a serving dish into a cone-shaped mound. Chill 1 hour. Whip the cream; fold the cognac into it. Completely cover the mound.

SERVES : 6–8

Budino di Ricotta

CHEESE–ALMOND PUDDING

1 pound ricotta cheese or ½ pound cream cheese and ½ pound cottage cheese
5 egg yolks
⅔ cup sugar
⅔ cup ground blanched almonds
⅓ cup chopped candied orange peel
2 teaspoons grated lemon rind

Run the cheese in an electric blender or force through a sieve. Beat the egg yolks and sugar until light, then beat in the cheese, almonds, orange peel and lemon rind. Turn into a buttered 7-inch spring form. Bake in a preheated 325° oven 45 minutes. Cool thoroughly before removing from spring-form.

SERVES : 4–6

Crema di Mascherpone

CHILLED CHEESE DESSERT

1 pound Mascherpone, ricotta or cream cheese
½ cup sugar
4 egg yolks, beaten
2 tablespoons heavy cream
2 tablespoons cognac
Raspberries or strawberries

Run the cheese in an electric blender until very smooth or force through a sieve. Beat in the sugar, egg yolks, cream and cognac, beating until very smooth and thick. Pour into a serving dish and chill. Garnish with raspberries or strawberries.

SERVES : 4–6

Crema Fritta

FRIED CREAM DESSERT

4 egg yolks
¼ cup sugar
½ cup sifted flour
⅛ teaspoon salt
4 cups milk, scalded
2 teaspoons grated orange or lemon rind
1 egg, beaten
½ cup dry bread crumbs
2 tablespoons vegetable oil
2 tablespoons butter

Beat the egg yolks and sugar in a double boiler. Cook over low heat, stirring constantly with a wooden spoon until slightly thickened. Mix in half the flour, the salt, and very gradually the milk. Cook, stirring steadily until very thick. At no time let the mixture boil. Mix in the rind. Rinse a square dish or pan with cold water and pour the mixture into it to a depth of 2 inches. Chill until firm. Cut into diamond shapes or squares.

Dip in the remaining flour, the egg and finally the bread crumbs. Heat the oil and butter in a skillet; brown the cream in it gently on both sides. Don't crowd the skillet. Serve sprinkled with sugar.

SERVES : 4–6

Plombières di Castagne

FROZEN CHESTNUT DESSERT

4 eggs
⅓ cup sugar
2 cups milk, scalded
1½ cups canned crème de marrons (chestnut purée)
2 tablespoons cognac
1 cup heavy cream

In the top of a double boiler, beat the eggs and sugar. Add the hot milk gradually, stirring steadily to prevent curdling. Place over hot, not boiling, water, and cook, stirring constantly until thickened. Remove from the heat; beat in the marrons and cognac. Chill for 3 hours.

Whip the cream and fold into the chestnut mixture. Heap on a serving dish and freeze for 2 hours.

SERVES : 6–8

Torrone Gelato

CHILLED NOUGAT PUDDING

6 hard-cooked egg yolks
4 tablespoons butter
⅓ cup sugar
2 tablespoons rum
3 tablespoons maraschino (cherry liqueur)
24 lady fingers, split
¾ cup Marsala or sweet sherry
2 tablespoons unsweetened cocoa

Mash the egg yolks with an electric mixer or with a wooden spoon. Add the butter, beating until very fluffy and light. Gradually beat in the sugar, again until very light. This should take about 3 minutes with an electric mixer, or 10 with a wooden spoon. Beat in the rum very gradually, then the maraschino. Beat again until very smooth and light.

Soak the lady fingers in the Marsala. Line the bottom of an oblong mold or pan with half the lady fingers. Spread with half the cream mixture. Beat the cocoa into the remaining half, and spread over the cream mixture. Cover with remaining lady fingers. Chill for 6 hours or overnight. Turn out onto a serving dish. Decorate with whipped cream, if desired.

SERVES : 6–8

Gelato di Fragole

STRAWBERRY ICE CREAM

1 cup sugar
¼ cup orange juice
1 tablespoon lemon juice
¾ cup water
2 quarts strawberries
1 cup heavy cream

Cook the sugar, orange juice, lemon juice and water, stirring steadily to the boiling point, then cook 5 minutes longer, or until syrupy. Cool.

Purée the berries in an electric blender, or force through a sieve. When the syrup is cool, mix it with the berries. Whip the cream and fold it in. Turn into two dry ice trays or into a mold. Cover. Put in the freezer for 4–5 hours or until firm.

SERVES : 6–8

Biscuit Tortoni

1½ cups heavy cream
½ cup sifted confectioners' sugar
3 tablespoons rum or cognac
1 egg white, stiffly beaten
½ cup chopped toasted almonds

Whip the cream until it begins to thicken, then gradually beat in the sugar until stiff. Stir in the rum or cognac. Fold in the egg white.

Spoon into eight to ten 2-3 inch paper cups; sprinkle with the almonds. Freeze 4 hours or until firm.

SERVES : 8–10

Frittatine Zingarella

PEAR–MERINGUE PANCAKES

Pear Filling:

1 pound pears, peeled and cubed
½ cup sugar

Cook the pears and sugar over low heat until very thick and dry. Cool.

Pancakes:

3 egg yolks
¾ cup milk
¾ cup water
1 tablespoon sugar
3 tablespoons cognac
1½ cups sifted flour
¼ teaspoon salt
¼ cup melted butter
2 tablespoons vegetable oil
2 tablespoons butter

Beat the egg yolks. Mix in the milk and water, then the sugar, cognac, then the flour and salt until very smooth. Stir in the butter. (If you have an electric blender, combine all the ingredients and blend until smooth.) Chill 2 hours.

Heat a little oil and butter in a 6 inch skillet; pour in enough batter to just coat the pan. Cook until delicately browned on both sides. Stack while preparing the balance. Place a tablespoon of the pear mixture on each pancake and roll up. Arrange in a buttered baking dish.

Meringue:

2 egg whites
¼ cup sugar

Beat the egg whites until soft peaks form, then very gradually beat in the sugar until very stiff. Heap over the pancakes. Bake in a preheated 450° oven 5 minutes or until delicately browned.

MAKES : 12 PANCAKES

Pesche Ripiene

STUFFED BAKED PEACHES

6 large firm peaches
2 tablespoons butter
1½ tablespoons sugar
¾ cup macaroon crumbs
1 egg yolk, beaten
1 tablespoon cognac
4 tablespoons Marsala or sweet sherry
¼ cup water

Peel the peaches, cut in half and remove the pits. Scoop out a little of the pulp to enlarge hollow. Mash the pulp.

Cream the butter and sugar together; mix in the crumbs, peach pulp, egg yolk and cognac. Stuff the peaches. Arrange in a buttered baking dish and sprinkle 1 teaspoon of the wine on each. Pour the water into the dish. Bake in a 350° oven 25 minutes or until peaches are tender but still firm.

SERVES : 6–12

Note: Canned cling peaches may be prepared in the same manner, but bake only 15 minutes.

Crema d'Ananas

PINEAPPLE PARFAIT

6 egg yolks
½ cup sugar
⅛ cup cognac
2 cups heavy cream
½ cup crushed drained canned pineapple

Beat the egg yolks and sugar in the top of a double boiler. Place over hot water and cook, stirring constantly, until thick and frothy. Remove from heat and stir in the cognac. Chill 2 hours.

Whip the cream and fold into the yolk mixture with the pineapple. Spoon into eight to ten parfait glasses or sherbet cups. Chill 2 hours before serving.

SERVES : 8–10

Omelette alla Fiamma

APRICOT FLAMING OMELET

4 egg yolks
¼ teaspoon salt
4 egg whites, stiffly beaten
2 tablespoons butter
4 tablespoons apricot jam
2 tablespoons confectioners' sugar
3 tablespoons warm cognac

Beat the egg yolks and salt until light. Fold in the egg whites. Melt the butter in a 9 or 10-inch skillet; pour in the egg mixture. Cook over low heat until bottom is delicately browned. Bake in a preheated 400° oven 5 minutes or until set and top browned. Spread with the jam. Roll up onto a heated serving dish. Sprinkle with the sugar. Place under the broiler to glaze.

Pour the cognac over the omelet and set aflame.

SERVES : 3–4

Pere Cotte Rosse

BAKED PEARS IN RED WINE

8 firm pears
1⅛ cups sugar
½ teaspoon grated lemon rind
4 cups dry red wine

Peel the pears, but leave stem on. Mix together the sugar, lemon rind and wine in a baking dish. Place the pears in it. Cover dish and bake in a 350° oven 50 minutes or until pears are tender but firm. Baste and turn pears frequently. Chill.

SERVES : 8

Note: White wine may be substituted for the red, in which case the dish is called Pere Cotte Bianche.

Torte

CAKES

$\mathbb{C}$ake- and pastry-making, as we know it, began with the Italians. The gastronomic arts developed at the same time that the city-state of Venice was at its peak of power. Venetians were rich, the richest group of people in all of Europe, and they turned their minds to fine foods and wines. Banquets held in 13th-century Venice were remarkable affairs that went on for hours, occasionally even for days. The marriage of the children of two prosperous families of Venice was an occasion that brought forth displays of the greatest skills of the cooks and chefs of the city.

It was during this period, for the first time, that specialists in the kitchen arts first appeared. The first meat chefs, the first cake-makers came into being at that time, for so involved had the culinary art of Italy become, that only specialists could hope to create the complicated creations which Venetians expected.

Cake-making is still regarded in Italy as a fine art, calling for the utmost devotion by its practitioners. Any person, man or woman, with a light hand in pastry-making is highly regarded by his neighbors.

211

Torta Mascherpone con Strega

CHEESE LAYER CAKE

¾ pound Mascherpone, ricotta or cream cheese
½ cup very fine granulated sugar
3 egg yolks
5 tablespoons Strega (orange liqueur)
4 tablespoons finely grated unsweetened chocolate
1 8-inch sponge cake, homemade or commercial
¼ cup water
1 cup heavy cream
Cinnamon

Beat the cheese and sugar until light, then beat in the egg yolks until fluffy. Remove half the mixture, and to the other half mix in 3 tablespoons Strega and the chocolate.

Split the sponge cake in half, making two 1-inch layers. Place one layer in a deep dish. Mix the remaining Strega with the water and pour over the layer. Spread the plain cheese mixture on it, then the chocolate. Cover with the sponge layer. Chill several hours. Whip the cream, and spread over the cake. Sprinkle with a little cinnamon.

SERVES : 6–8

Pane di Spagna

SPONGE CAKE

1¼ cups sifted flour
¼ teaspoon salt
¼ teaspoon ground anise (optional)
8 egg yolks
2 tablespoons cold water
1¼ cups fine granulated sugar
2 tablespoons grated orange rind
8 egg whites

Sift together three times the flour, salt, and anise.

Beat the egg yolks and water; gradually beat in ¾ cup sugar until light and fluffy. Fold in the flour mixture and orange rind.

Beat the egg whites until soft peaks form; gradually beat in the remaining sugar until stiff but not dry. Fold into the flour mixture. Turn into an ungreased 9-inch tube pan. Bake in a preheated 350° oven 50 minutes or until browned and shrunk away from side of pan. Invert on a cake rack and let cool in the pan. Run a spatula around the sides and center tube and turn cake out.

Note: The batter may be baked in two 9-inch or three 8-inch layer cake pans. Bake 9-inch pans 30 minutes, 8-inch 25 minutes.

S E R V E S : 8–10

Gató di Castagne

CHESTNUT REFRIGERATOR TORTE

1 pound chestnuts
2 eggs
½ cup sugar
2 cups milk
1 square (ounce) unsweetened chocolate
3 tablespoons cognac
1 teaspoon vanilla extract
1 cup heavy cream

Cut a crisscross in the pointed end of the chestnuts. Cover with water, bring to a boil and cook over low heat 40 minutes. Drain, cool slightly, peel and remove inner skin. Purée the chestnuts in an electric blender or force through a sieve. Beat the eggs and sugar in the top of a double boiler. Stir in the milk and the chocolate, broken into small pieces. Place over hot water and cook, stirring constantly until thickened. Beat in the chestnuts, 1 tablespoon cognac, and the vanilla. Cool slightly, then turn into a well greased 7-inch tube pan. Chill 4 hours or until firm. Carefully unmold onto a serving dish. Fill center with the cream, whipped, and flavored with remaining cognac.

S E R V E S : 6–8

Pasta Sfogliata

ITALIAN PUFF PASTE

Pastry:

2 cups flour
¼ teaspoon salt
1 tablespoon lemon juice
½ cup ice water
½ pound sweet butter

Sift the flour and salt into a bowl; make a well in the center; into it put the lemon juice and the ice water. Work in flour until a dough is formed. Knead the dough on a lightly-floured surface about 10 minutes. Add a little flour if dough is too sticky. Wrap in a towel and chill 30 minutes.

Roll out the dough into a rectangle ½-inch thick. Form the butter into a flat cake and put it in the center of the dough. Fold over one side, then the other. Press open edges at top and bottom together. Roll dough into a rectangle, and fold over into thirds again. Wrap in the towel and chill 15 minutes. Repeat rolling, folding and chilling four more times, always facing the open ends (those not folded over) towards you. Use for making pastries.

Cheese Filling:

1 pound ricotta cheese
¼ cup sugar
¾ cup chopped candied fruit
¼ cup ground almonds
1 tablespoon grated orange rind
2 egg whites, stiffly beaten

Roll out half the dough to fit an 11-inch pie plate. Chill while preparing the filling.

Beat the cheese and sugar until smooth. Mix in the candied fruits, almonds and orange rind. Fold in the egg whites. Spread in the lined pie plate. Roll out the remaining dough and cover the pan, pressing the edges together. Bake in a preheated 400° oven 30 minutes. Cool on a cake rack.

SERVES : 8–10

Amaretti

MACAROONS

2 egg whites
¼ teaspoon salt
1 cup sugar
1 cup ground blanched almonds
1 teaspoon almond extract

Beat the egg whites and salt until frothy. Gradually beat in the sugar until stiff but not dry. Fold in the almonds and almond extract.

Rinse a cooky sheet with cold water but do not dry it. Drop the mixture onto it by the teaspoon, leaving 1 inch between each. Bake in a preheated 325° oven 20 minutes or until delicately browned and dry. Remove with a spatula.

MAKES : ABOUT 2½ DOZEN

Biscottini Deliziosi

MERINGUE CRISPS

3 tablespoons butter
½ cup sugar
½ teaspoon vanilla extract
¼ cup heavy cream
2½ tablespoons flour
3 egg whites, beaten stiff

Cream the butter; gradually beat in the sugar until light. Beat in the vanilla and cream, then mix in the flour. Fold in the egg whites, mixing until a dough is formed. Pat out on a lightly-floured surface and cut into strips 2-inches long by ¼-inch wide. Arrange on a greased cooky sheet, leaving space between each, as they spread in baking. Bake in a preheated 450° oven 5 minutes, or until delicately browned. Cool on a cake rack.

MAKES : ABOUT 3 DOZEN

Sfinge

CRULLERS

2 cups sifted flour
¼ teaspoon salt
3 teaspoons baking powder
½ teaspoon mace
2 eggs
½ cup sugar
1 tablespoon vegetable oil
⅓ cup milk
Vegetable oil for deep frying
Powdered sugar

Sift together the flour, salt, baking powder, and mace. Beat the eggs, sugar, and oil until thick. Stir in the milk, then the flour mixture. Beat until very smooth. Cover with a towel and let stand 15 minutes.

Heat the fat to 370°. Drop the batter into it by the tablespoon, a few at a time. Fry until browned, about 4 minutes. Remove with a slotted spoon and drain. Sprinkle with sugar, flavored with anise, if you like.

MAKES : ABOUT 3 DOZEN

Tortelli di San Giuseppe

FRIED PUFFS

2 cups sifted flour
1 teaspoon baking powder
2 tablespoons yellow cornmeal
1 tablespoon sugar
1 egg, beaten
¼ teaspoon salt
½ cup water
½ cup milk
Vegetable oil for deep frying
Confectioners' sugar

Sift the flour, baking powder, cornmeal and sugar into a bowl. Mix in the egg, salt, water and milk; beat until very smooth.

Heat the oil to 370°. Drop the mixture into it by the teaspoon. Fry until puffed and browned. Don't crowd the pan. Drain on absorbent paper. Sprinkle with confectioners' sugar. Serve hot or cold.

MAKES : ABOUT 3½ DOZEN

Cenci

FRIED CRISPS

2 cups flour
¼ teaspoon salt
2 teaspoons baking powder
3 eggs
2 tablespoons sugar
1 tablespoon vegetable oil
1 teaspoon almond extract
Fat for deep drying
Confectioners' sugar

Sift together the flour, salt and baking powder. Beat the eggs, sugar, oil and almond extract until thick. Beat in the flour mixture, then turn out onto a floured surface. Knead until smooth. (If too soft, add a little more flour.) Cover with a bowl and let stand 1 hour.

Divide the dough into 2 pieces. Roll out each piece paper-thin. Use a fluted pastry wheel or very sharp knife and cut into ¾-inch wide strips, 5 inches long. Let stand 10 minutes. Heat the fat to 370°. Fry a few pieces at a time until puffed and browned, about 2 minutes. Drain well and sprinkle with confectioners' sugar.

MAKES : ABOUT 3 DOZEN

Vino, Vino, Vino!

When I opened my first restaurant in California, the majority of Americans knew about only one Italian wine, Chianti. This popular wine, undoubtedly the most famous one in the world, may be found in all parts of the world, from the largest and most sophisticated cities to the smallest hamlets in the remotest corners of the world. Some friends of mine, off on a big-game hunt in Africa, reported that when they ultimately encountered a native village with its equivalent of a general store, there are sure to be bottles of Chianti for sale. Because of the wine's acceptance, when I opened my restaurant in Beverly Hills, I named it the Chianti.

But what remarkable things have happened in the score of years that have passed! European travel has become so commonplace that many Americans are as familiar with the tourist attractions of Italy as they are with those of their homeland. They have traveled through the smallest villages of Italy, sampling the local food and wines as they wandered. Americans have developed a great liking for Italian food, and it is a rare city in the United States, regardless of size, that does not have its Italian restaurant. In addition, they have learned a great deal about Italian wines, and now knowingly order a bottle of Barolo wine with a steak, and a cooled Soave with fish. For all of this increased knowledge,

219

I am very happy indeed, because I want as many Americans as possible to learn about the delights of Italian wines.

Wine is an extremely personal experience, meaning a different thing to each person. Wine, being a natural and healthy beverage, has so great an acceptance in Italy that water is seldom served, and a meal without wine is almost unthinkable. Wine has become so important because of its delicious taste, and the peculiar talent it possesses for enhancing the flavor of food. Because, basically, that is the purpose of wine—to accompany food and improve its taste.

Think of any drink in the world, including both soft and hard liquors, including coffee, tea, cocoa, milk, fruit juices, scotch, rye, bourbon, vodka, cola drinks and so forth. Once you have tasted grapefruit juice, for example, it is reasonable to assume that all the grapefruit juice consumed during the remainder of your life will taste just about the same; the same logic would apply to all other drinks. But wine—that is something entirely different. By its nature, wine changes just a little as it matures within the bottle, so that although still retaining its original qualities, the wine is somewhat different from one month to another. Furthermore, not all wines are similar, even before being bottled. Thus, the curious wine-drinker is presented with an entire world of wines from which to choose. That, too, explains why a wine-drinker will select a heavy wine today, and perhaps a lighter one tomorrow. Because wines, too, have their own personality and what suits us on a particular day may not suit us on another.

At my restaurant, therefore, there is a choice available from among 40 or more wines. Some wines, of course, are more suitable with certain foods than are others. Most wine-drinkers acknowledge that white wines taste best with fish and red wines with meat, and this basic principle is not merely a matter of individual opinion, but one that has developed over a period of a thousand years or more by millions of wine-drinkers the world over. Many wine merchants, perhaps anxious to sell more wines to an increased public, have begun to say that if you like white wine with roast beef, by all means drink it. Also, that any wine is suitable with any food, if *you* like it. With this, I must disagree. In the long run, the potential wine-drinker will ultimately tire of his wrong combination, and cease to be a wine-drinker. The rules of drinking wine are so simple that anyone can memorize them in a matter of a minute, and always order the correct wine. Repeating the basic premise that white wines are best with fish, and red wines with red meat, this leaves merely a few points of discussion. Chicken and veal, both white meats, may be accompanied by a white wine, or if you wish, by a light red wine; this is a matter of personal preference. Also, a seafood served in a red sauce, like lobster *fra* diavolo, is equally good with red or white wines.

Most of the food served in my restaurant is prepared in what might be called northern Italian-style, to differentiate it from the southern style. In general, southern-style food has more garlic and herbs, makes a greater use of tomatoes, and in general, is a somewhat more highly-spiced style of cuisine. Northern Italian food is lighter and more delicate, tending to use butter rather than making exclusive use of olive oil. For some reason, nature has arranged in an unfathomable manner that the wines of northern Italy best accompany northern Italian food. The same peculiar principle holds true in France, for French food is perfect with French wines; French food would not be nearly so good with Italian wines. It is only natural that most of the wines in my restaurant are northern wines, produced from Rome northward to the borders of Italy that touch Austria and Switzerland. However, certain dishes which originated in southern Italy, particularly some of the marvelous *pastas*, have become so popular all over Italy, that they have become a part of the national cuisine; in the same way, an American southern dish, fried chicken, is served all over the United States. Inasmuch as a few southern-style dishes appear on my menu, a few wines of southern Italy are available in my restaurant, because they best accompany the hearty, fully-flavored dishes of that part of Italy.

Needless to say, the choice of wines is entirely individual, and any selection of them must be a matter of opinion and an expression of one's own personality. But, as I am very fond of wines and extremely interested in them, I have devoted a great deal of time and attention to my wine list. Of course, no one could fail to include such standbys as Valpolicella, Barolo, Bardolino, Frascati, Chianti and the like. However, I take pride in my wine list, because I believe that it represents the very best that Italy has to offer. As I mentioned before, although most of the wines are northern in origin, there is a representative sprinkling of the best from the south, including Naples and Sicily.

Here is a brief description of the wines which are served in my restaurant:

Red Wines

Barbaresco: From the neighborhood of Turin comes this somewhat light wine, similar to Barolo in nature, but even smoother when fully mature. It has about 12½ to 14% alcohol, and many people claim they can find the taste of almonds in this wine.

Barbera: A ruby-colored wine, with a full-bodied flavor, averaging from 12 to 15% alcohol. It has a pleasing bouquet, and is very good with red meats.

Bardolino: This bright, crystal-clear wine comes from the shores of beautiful Lake Garda. It has a fruity taste, sometimes accompanied by small, prickling bubbles, and it tastes best when rather young.

Barolo: One of Italy's finest wines, and worthy of everyone's attention. Barolo averages from 13–15% alcohol; when young it is full-bodied and delicious. When about eight years old, it develops some remarkably fine characteristics, with a so-called "violet" taste, and becomes reminiscent of a Rhône wine, particularly Hermitage.

Chianti: This world-renowned wine requires some explanation. It is produced in enormous quantities in Tuscany, principally around the art city of Florence, and is the sort of wine that can be drunk in large gulps, rather than sipped, being very "drinkable" in nature. It is a blend of three or four different types of grapes, with from 11 to 13.5% alcohol. The one type known the world over is the characteristic squat bottle covered with woven straw, called a *fiasco,* or flask. Without this straw, the bottle could not be placed upon the table, for it has a rounded bottom. When young, the wine is fruity and has a fresh, appealing taste. When aged, however, the wine becomes more sedate and self-important, developing a well-rounded, characteristic quality far removed from the youthful nature of Chianti bottled in a *fiasco.* The aged wine is called Chianti Classico, and is shipped to the market in a regular wine bottle, without the straw covering. There is a Chianti called Riserva Ducale, about five or more years old, that is exceptionally good. However, any Chianti which bears the mark of Antinori, Bertolli, Brolio, Melini, Olivieri or Ruffino is sure to be of high quality.

Falerno: A ruby-red wine produced near Naples, with about 12% alcohol. It is not always a completely dry wine, but it is distinguished by its fine bouquet which seems to rise from the glass.

Freisa: This wine comes from the neighborhood of Turin, and is of somewhat low alcoholic content, averaging 11–12%. When young, the wine seems somehow a bit rough to the palate, but when three or more years old, it develops a fine body. Many people find in it a vague taste of raspberries.

Gattinara: A garnet-colored wine with unusual highlights, produced near Lake Maggiore. It has from 11 to 13% alcohol, and is fairly good when young; after about three years, it becomes progressively smoother and aristocratic. Many people regard it as one of Italy's finest wines, although it is but little-known in the United States.

Grignolino: This light, ruby-red wine comes from near Turin. It has a variable alcoholic content, ranging from 11 to 14%, and is known for its very fresh taste, with a slight undertone of bitterness. It is a very good, distinctive wine.

Inferno: This wine is produced near the Swiss border, in vineyards planted on steep hillsides. It is bright and ruby red, averaging 12½% alcohol, and has a sturdy, manly quality. The bouquet is especially pleasant.

Lambrusco di Sorbara: Produced near the food capital of Italy—Bologna—Lambrusco is fairly low in alcohol (10–12%), sometimes quite dry, sometimes a little sweet. It has a lovely purple cast, a fruity taste, and is often slightly sparkling.

Montepulciano: A wine grown and made near the historic city of Siena, with from 11 to 14% alcohol. Only fair when young, after three years, it develops a mellow quality with a vaguely bitter (but not unpleasant) taste.

Nebbiolo: A light, ruby-red wine, with 12–13% alcohol, and a pleasing dry quality, making it ideal with *pasta* dishes; when older, it is an excellent accompaniment to roast meats.

Reccioto: A little-known wine in the United States, Reccioto is produced around historic Verona, and is often called Reccioto Veronese. It is rather sweet and has a smooth, velvety taste.

Santa Maddalena: Produced in mountainous Bolzano, near the Austrian border, this wine is quite dry, with a slightly bitter aftertaste, much prized by connoisseurs.

Sassella: A fruity, fresh wine with a bright ruby-red color, averaging 12½% alcoholic content. The bouquet is particularly unusual, and the wine is very full-bodied and satisfying.

Valpantena: A Veronese wine, much like its better-known neighbor, Valpolicella. It is a very bright, red color, with from 10½ to 13% alcohol, but is somewhat lighter in body than Valpolicella.

Valpolicella: A distinctive wine with a most pleasing body and bouquet, often regarded as the Italian wine most like a French wine. The wine has an almost ideal combination of taste, aroma, and bouquet. All in all, one of the best wines of Italy.

White Wines

Asprinio: A dry white wine, perfect with fish dishes, and known for its peculiar sparkling quality. It is produced in Aversa, near Naples.

Brolio Bianco: A truly excellent dry wine, made around Siena, with a remarkable, fresh, crisp taste. An all-around white wine, particularly clean and refreshing to the palate; quite exceptional.

Capri: A dry wine, with an attractive straw color and a fresh taste. At one time, most of the wine was actually made on this attractive little island, but as land values have climbed skyward, much of Capri wine is now being made around the Bay of Naples.

Corvo: From Palermo, in Sicily, comes this moderately dry white wine, with its unusual gold color. It averages 12% alcohol, and is quite pleasant.

Est! Est!! Est!!! A yellowish wine with an extremely pleasing bouquet. It is somewhat sweet, and has a pronounced flavor of Muscat, making it rather fruity to the taste.

Fontana Candida: From Frascati, comes this wine of the Castelli Romani, a district just to the southeast of Rome. It is the daily, everyday white wine of the Romans; it has a gold color and is rather dry.

Lagrima d'Arno: An extremely dry white wine, averaging 11% alcohol, with a pleasant yellowish color. It is produced in Tuscany, through which runs the renowned Arno River, and thus bears its name, The Tears of the Arno.

Lagrima Christi: Sometimes also called Lacrima Christi, this is an amber-colored wine with a light and somewhat fruity taste. It is not completely dry, having a slightly sweet quality.

Orvieto: A very clear, pale-gold wine reaching the market in straw-covered bottles like Chianti. The wine may be either dry (*secco*) or moderately sweet (*abboccato*), but the dry type is far better.

Prosecco: A sparkling white wine with a golden cast, having a dry to moderately sweet taste. It has an unusual quality, being pleasingly bitter, with a high percentage of tannic acid.

Soave: A straw-colored wine, with a vague green undertone; it averages about 11% alcohol. Produced near Lake Garda, a dry, well-balanced wine having a fine, full body. Best when very young.

Valtellina: A dry white wine, having about 11½% alcohol, produced in Lombardy, northern Italy, near the village of Sondrio. It is very light in body, almost ethereally so.

Verdicchio: An unusual white wine, made from a comparatively rare type of grape. The wine is shipped in distinctively-shaped bottles resembling an amphora; it has a spicy, dryish quality.

Rosato (Pink) Wines

Antinori Rosé: A pleasing light *rosé* wine, ideal during warm weather; has a clean aftertaste.

Rosatello Ruffino: A very light fruity, pink wine, suitable with almost all kinds of food; it has a beautiful color.

Chiaretto del Garda: Another pink wine produced along the shores of lovely Lake Garda; the wine is light, pleasant and quite low in alcohol.

Dessert Wines and After-Dinner Drinks

Malvasia: An interesting sweet white dessert wine, produced on the island of Stromboli, off the northeast coast of Sicily. It has an attractive golden yellow color and is made from dried, rather than fresh grapes.

Marsala: Sicily's greatest wine, prepared in dry, medium or sweet types. It is fortified with additional alcohol, and may be roughly compared to sherry or Madeira.

Asti Spumante: A sparkling white wine, often erroneously compared to champagne, for it has a different and distinctive quality of its own. Asti Spumante is delicious after dinner, being quite sweet, with a most pleasing fruity taste of Muscat grapes.

Aleatico: On Napoleon's island of Elba, they produce this excellent sweet red dessert wine, averaging almost 15% alcohol. Aleatico is famed for its remarkable bouquet.

Bracchetto: A cherry-red wine, low in alcohol (about 9%) but quite sweet, making it ideal for after-dinner. It is extraordinarily smooth and velvety.

Strega: A renowned Italian after-dinner liqueur, with an orange flavored base, and a bitter-sweet taste; it is something like yellow Chartreuse.

Aurum: An orange-flavored cordial with herbs added.

Cerasella: A cherry liqueur; remarkably fresh fruit taste.

Ratafia: An unusual after-dinner liqueur made from a variety of fruits and nuts.

Italian Title Index

229

Recipe Index

almond:
  cheese pudding, 202–203
  cream mold, 201
anchovies:
  and sausages with cabbage, 181
  on toast, 13
anchovy dip, hot, 16
apricot flaming omelet, 209
artichoke pie, 18
artichokes:
  with butter and cheese, 178
  deviled, Roman style, 177
  with lamb and egg sauce, 117–118
  Roman-style, 178–179
  stuffed, with tuna, 3–4
  and veal, 119
  and veal casserole, 128
asparagus:
  with parmesan cheese, 179
  soup, cream of, 35–36

bass, striped:
  with mushroom-wine sauce, 44–45
  in olive sauce, 45–46
  in tomato sauce, 44
bean:
  and escarole soup, 22–23
  and macaroni soup, 32
  soup, 31
  soup, Genoa style, 32–33
  and tuna fish appetizer, 18
beans:
  green, with ham, 180
  green, in tomato sauce, 179–180
  lima, with ham, 180–181
  with rice, mountaineer's style, 94
  and smoked beef, 14
  Tuscan-style, 11
  white, and caviar, 12
beef:
  baked, 111
  birds, 108–109

boiled mixed meats, 115
Bolognese sauce, 170
braised, in red wine, 114
broth with pastina, 26
dried, and melon, 15
dried, stuffed, 15
eggplant-meat casserole, 185–186
fillet of:
  with pâté, 108
  with pepper sauce, 106
  sautéed, in wine, 106–107
  with shallot sauce, 104–105
  split, with rosemary and brandy, 104
  stuffed, 107
  in vermouth, 105
liver, see calf's liver
meat sauce, 170–171
meat-ball sauce, 171–172
oxtails, braised, 144–145
with parsley sauce, 109
roast, marinated, 112–113
smoked, and beans, 14
steak, Florentine style, 110
steak in tomato sauce, 110–111
stuffed, 113–114
tartar, 13–14
with white wine, 112
biscuit tortoni, 206
brain croquettes, 139
brains:
  breaded, Milan fashion, 138–139
  in brown butter, 138
  mixed fried foods, 50–51
broccoli and macaroni soup, 29

cabbage:
  with anchovies and sausages, 181
  and rice, Lombardy style, 92
cake, see also torte:
  cheese layer, 212
  sponge, 212–213

233